FAITH MISUSED

WHY CHRISTIANITY IS NOT JUST ANOTHER RELIGION

ALVIN J. SCHMIDT

CONCORDIA PUBLISHING HOUSE · SAINT LOUIS

To my sons, Tim and Mark,
and grandsons, J. P. and Will

Published by Concordia Publishing House
3558 S. Jefferson Avenue, St. Louis, MO 63118-3968
1-800-325-3040 • cph.org

Manufactured in the United States of America

Library of Congress Cataloging-in-Publication Data

Names: Schmidt, Alvin J., author.

Title: Faith misused : why Christianity is not just another religion / Alvin J Schmidt.

Description: Saint Louis, MO : Concordia Publishing House, [2022] | Summary: "Overview of the use of the Greek word pistis in the New Testament and how the English word faith is often misused"-- Provided by publisher.

Identifiers: LCCN 2021042749 (print) | LCCN 2021042750 (ebook) | ISBN 9780758671110 (paperback) | ISBN 9780758671127 (ebook)

Subjects: LCSH: Faith. | Faith--Biblical teaching.

Classification: LCC BT771.3 .S35 2021 (print) | LCC BT771.3 (ebook) | DDC 234/.23--dc23

LC record available at https://lccn.loc.gov/2021042749

LC ebook record available at https://lccn.loc.gov/2021042750

---

1 2 3 4 5 6 7 8 9 10   31 30 29 28 27 26 25 24 23 22

PRAISE FOR *FAITH MISUSED*

Alvin Schmidt is a genuine national treasure and one of our most prescient intellectuals in the public square. Decade upon decade, he has produced mini masterpieces that have predicated massive shifts in public policy and conscience, all reasoned from his faith-informed scholarship and lyrical pen. He has done it again in *Faith Misused*, a book so timely, topical, and relevant that we are almost morally obliged to benefit from its vision and scope.

Timothy S. Goeglein, Vice President, Focus on the Family, Washington, DC

With the careful research and attention to theological detail that we have come to expect from him, Alvin Schmidt teaches the faithful to rejoice in and safeguard the treasure that is the word faith. After reading this volume, no one will glibly speak of faith outside of its biblical, Christian usage. For those who confess sola fide, the insights of Schmidt's latest work cannot be ignored.

Rev. Dr. Kevin S. Golden, author of *Blessed Be His Name*,
associate professor of exegetical theology, Concordia Seminary, St. Louis

A quarter century ago, Prince Charles announced that as king he would be "defender of faith"—removing the definite article from the title that English monarchs have borne since Henry VIII attacked Luther. Alvin Schmidt definitively restores the article in this remarkable little book. Christianity is *the* faith, the one and only. Any other "faithing" is in vain because it's like grasping at breath on a cold morning or trying to stand on a cloud. There's nothing there. But the true faith finds its firm foundation in Christ, the rock.

Rev. Dr. Thomas M. Winger, President, Concordia Lutheran
Theological Seminary, St. Catharines, Ontario, Canada

During my theological training at seminary (admittedly decades ago!), not a single professor made me aware of the basic thesis of Dr. Schmidt's book: that there is just one faith, not a plethora of "faiths." That is, there is a variety of religions in the world but only a single faith. I, along with the majority of twenty-first-century scholars, would speak of other "faiths," but Dr. Schmidt shows me the error of my thinking and speaking. I recommend Dr. Schmidt's book to any readers who want to do a historical cleanup of their own thinking and speaking as Christians.

Dr. Rod Rosenbladt, professor emeritus of theology and Christian apologetics, Concordia University Irvine

Words matter. A lot. Some false words, as Plato taught, are infectious with evil, corrupting all who use them with their lies. In *Faith Misused*, Alvin Schmidt traces the story of a grand deception, the subversion of the word *faith*. He takes the reader on a compelling journey through the history of ideas, tracing the course of this deception, and finishes with a clarion call for the biblical meaning of *faith* to be restored in our day. This book speaks to the heart of every Christian's faith.

Mark Durie, Senior Research Fellow, Melbourne School of Theology, and director of the Institute for Spiritual Awareness

CONTENTS

FOREWORD

Some years ago, Dr. Norman Nagel, of blessed memory, was a guest on Todd Wilken's wonderful radio program *Issues, Etc.* Wilken asked Dr. Nagel to talk about faith. Nagel responded, "No." Wilken was taken aback and politely asked again, "Dr. Nagel, would you tell us what faith is?" "I will not," replied Nagel again, to his somewhat perplexed host. "But I will talk about Christ, who is the content of faith."

I couldn't help but think of this incident while perusing the pages of this latest work by Alvin Schmidt, *Faith Misused*. The good doctor takes the reader on a trek through the history of the Church and popular Christianity, the latter of which is infused with the language of "faith" but has lost its content: Christ and the "faith that was . . . delivered to the saints" (Jude 3).

Why is this important? We Christians live in a cultural context in Western Christianity that is floundering in popular notions of comparative religions, philosophy, and liberal Christianity that has hijacked terms from Christianity but denied their very content. In fact, "faith" as used popularly today has nothing to do with its object, Christ and His gifts. We postmodern Christians all too easily appropriate these misappropriations and come to speak in ways that our orthodox Christian forebearers would not even recognize as Christian. And the less we speak like Christians, the less we shall be Christians.

Says Chad Walsh, as quoted in chapter 4 of this book, "Millions of Christians live in a sentimental haze of vague piety, with soft organ music trembling in lovely light from stained-glass windows. Their religion is a thing of pleasant emotional quivers, divorced from the will, divorced from the intellect, and demanding little except lip service to a few harmless platitudes." Amen.

The reader will never again speak in such a subjective, emotional, and finally meaningless manner about faith in the one "name under heaven given among men by which we must be saved" (Acts 4:12).

Matthew C. Harrison
President, The Lutheran Church—Missouri Synod

INTRODUCTION

This book focuses on the biblical concept of faith, specifically the Greek concept of *pistis* (faith) as found in the New Testament, which has been hijacked and misused in numerous books, articles, and spoken words. The book's first chapter, "Faith (*Pistis*), Exclusively Christian, but Largely Unknown," is the standard-bearer of the exclusive faith that was operative in the lives of the early Christians as revealed in the New Testament. The misuses of faith cited and discussed in this book are departures from that exclusive faith.

Since the Early Middle Ages, the exclusiveness of the faith that was present among Christians in the New Testament has been largely unknown, as countless books and articles (past and present) reveal when their authors discuss the religious concept of faith. Countless Christians, both laypeople and clergy, who have read and studied the New Testament are also unaware of the exclusive use and nature of faith in the New Testament.

The exclusivity of *pistis* (faith) and *pistis* language in the lives of Christians in the New Testament is, of course, not easily perceived, given that none of its twenty-seven books contains a declarative sentence that makes this exclusivity notably obvious. Thus, it requires discerning observation on the part of readers to consciously perceive that this faith in the New Testament is exclusively Christian. But this required perception did not occur to or register with Christian readers for centuries. This unfortunate fact compels me to share a personal experience.

For many years after I had successfully completed my studies at a Lutheran theological seminary, I enjoyed reading and studying the different books of the New Testament in English and in Greek. However, like many Christians and their pastors, I had never noticed that the Greek word *pistis* and the *pistis* language in the New Testament are always and only used with Christian meanings and applications. Not until some years later, after reading William Henry Paine Hatch's informative book *The Pauline Idea of Faith in Its Relation to Jewish and Hellenistic Religion* (published in 1917), did I learn that the New Testament introduced two innovative attributes of *pistis*: (1) the use of *pistis* as a religious principle, a status it did not previously have among the ancient Greeks, and (2) *pistis* as exclusively Christian, because its role and nature in the New Testament was applicable only to Christians. As Hatch noted, "Faith is the basic principle of Christianity and the distinguishing characteristic of Christians."[1]

Since Hatch's book in 1917, two New Testament scholars have further documented these findings: Dieter Lührmann, a German New Testament historian, and Teresa Morgan, a professor of Greco-Roman history at Oxford University, have also shown that *pistis* first became a religious principle in early Christianity and that *pistis* language never refers to anyone other than Christians in the New Testament. The citations of these scholars are noted and dis-

1 William Henry Paine Hatch, *The Pauline Idea of Faith in Its Relation to Jewish and Hellenistic Religion* (Cambridge, MA: Harvard University Press, 1917), 38.

cussed in the first chapter.[2] However, though these three scholars clearly show that faith (*pistis*) is Christianity's exclusive concept, they did not note that this unique reality is largely unknown and has been for centuries, including by most Christians.

Our syncretistic culture, however, does not like to hear the scholarly corroborations of the Christ-centered exclusive faith of the early Christians. To make known the nature of that exclusive faith is incompatible with the multicultural ideology that sees faith as present in all religions. Thus, this book's noting and underscoring the evidence of these scholarly citations in part reflects the spirit of the early Christians who, contrary to Rome's religiously syncretistic culture, unequivocally made their exclusive faith known publicly, which frequently resulted in persecution.

To aid readers' understanding of the exclusive faith of the early Christians, the book's first chapter documents how the concept of faith in the New Testament is anchored in the biblical, historical phenomena of Christ's crucifixion and His bodily resurrection made known and corroborated by His apostles' eyewitness accounts. These accounts prompted and sustained the faith of the early Christians, giving hope and meaning to Christ's promise of eternal life that could only be obtained through their faith in Him. This faith, together with their faith-motivated way of life, gave them a distinctive identity in the Greco-Roman world, where during the first three centuries of their church's existence, they were a despised religious minority of which many were persecuted and even executed.

2 These three scholars may not be the only ones who have noted that the word *pistis* and *pistis* language are exclusively Christian in the New Testament, but my research has not revealed any others.

The first chapter further notes that many authors who now write books and articles pertaining to Christianity's concept of faith depict it as a subjective phenomenon that lacks an evidential, historical foundation, a position clearly contrary to the New Testament's portrayal of faith. In contrast to the nature and the role of the faith found in the New Testament, these publications thus present readers with various misuses of faith, discussed later in the book.

Chapter 2 cites and discusses some renowned, prominent Bible critics who hijacked the exclusive faith of Christians from its biblical, historical foundation. These critics operated with the Enlightenment's presupposition that Christ's miracles and bodily resurrection were not authentic, historical events, for they regarded them as contrary to reason, the supreme value in Enlightenment philosophy. Given this radical action, the critics perceived orthodox-minded Christians would likely conclude their faith was therefore null and void. To calm perturbed and shocked Christians, the critics assured them that the purported miracles of Christ and His bodily resurrection were still valid if they, in sincere faith, believed these had really happened. The critics emphasized that the Christians' faith was what mattered, not whether the biblical accounts underlying their faith were factually true; the biblical accounts were merely a reflection of the "faith" of Christ's admiring apostles. In short, critics employing Enlightenment philosophy changed the prevailing understanding of faith—hijacking it from its biblical, historical source—resulting in widespread misuse and misunderstanding of the term to the present day.

The third chapter, "*Faith* and *Religion* Synonymized, Today's Popular Misuse of Faith," focuses on how Friedrich Schleiermacher, a liberal German theologian, introduced two other revolutionary misuses of the exclusive faith of Christians. Both misuses first appeared in his book *Der christliche Glaube* (The Christian Faith). The first misuse was when he synonymized the words *faith* and *religion*, an act that ascribed faith to any and every religion. This radical action nullified the exclusive nature and role of faith in the New Testament.

The second misuse began when Schleiermacher coined the German word *Glaubensweisen*, "faiths"—using *faith* in the plural. Like synonymizing *faith* and *religion*, pluralizing *faith* is also contrary to the New Testament, which uses *pistis* only in its singular form and applies it only to Christianity. The pluralizing of *faith* as *faiths* is now quite common in today's English-speaking world, so much so that the word *religions* is now increasingly not used, even when it would be more correct. The word *faiths* has largely preempted the word *religions*.

The third chapter further notes that the pluralization of *faith* resulted in countless individuals, including Christians, erroneously and ironically referring to other religions as "faiths." One frequently sees this misuse of faith by Christians in various Christian publications. By doing so, they deny, likely unwittingly, that the concept of *pistis* and *pistis* language in the New Testament refers only to Christians. Even many conservative Christian clergy now write and talk about other "faiths," as heard in sermons or seen in church publications.

Chapter 4, "From Faith to Fideism: A Deceptive Misuse of Faith," examines the varying hues of fideism (that is, having faith in faith itself) as seen in publications that discuss the topic of faith. When the Bible critics divorced faith from its biblical, historical foundation, faith became a concept no longer based on historically reliable evidence. This nonevidential view of faith is now widespread in many theologically liberal colleges, universities, and seminaries, as well as their publications. But sometimes it is now also found in print in some of the religious media in conservative and Evangelical circles.

The apostle Peter enjoined the first-century Christians to "always be ready to give a defense to everyone who asks you a reason for the hope that is in you, with meekness and fear" (1 Peter 3:15 NKJV). This passage, which expects Christians to defend their exclusive faith, may be one of the least-familiar or least-heeded references in the Bible. As chapter 4 documents, fideism sometimes appeals to devout Christians who tend to see faith as merely trusting what they believe without needing to cite any biblical defense or evidence.

The fifth chapter, "Idiosyncratic Views of Faith: The Subjective Misuse of Faith," discusses and critiques various idiosyncratic views of faith that largely echo eccentric or highly individualistic—and unbiblical—views of faith. Ordinarily, these would likely not be expressed by theologically well-informed individuals because idiosyncratic expressions of faith are highly subjective expressions. But they often receive public attention because they tend to be voiced by well-known individuals holding prominent or high-status positions, even though their views have no meaningful relevance to the nature and role of faith found in the New Testament. Thus, we find individuals saying, "Faith is irrational," "Faith has no business dealing with facts," "Faith is believing in the improbable," "Faith is mere folly," and the well-known cliché "Keep the faith" that is never defined.

Chapter 6, "'The Christian Faith': The Unrecognized Misuse of Faith," focuses on the appellation "the Christian faith." Many Christians have used and continue to use this phrase, unaware of its implications—namely, the idea that non-Christian religions also have and use faith, which is contrary to the New Testament's exclusively Christian use and meaning of faith.

After documenting with evidence from reputable scholars that the New Testament never uses the concept of *pistis* or *pistis* language to refer to anyone but Christians, this chapter urges Christians to stop using the phrase "the Christian faith" by regularly and consistently using the biblically compatible name "Christianity." Doing so, they will be reaffirming the New Testament's use of *pistis* (faith) as Christianity's exclusive concept.

The seventh chapter, "Equating Today's *Belief* with *Faith*, also a Misuse of Faith," discusses the long-held custom of English-speaking Christians of equating the words *belief* and *faith*. The chapter reviews how the meaning of each word changed over the years and discusses the differences between the Greek terms and the English equivalents. Then, the chapter ends with suggestions for more appropriate usages for Christians who want to convey the correct understanding of the New Testament's use of faith.

CHAPTER 1

FAITH (*PISTIS*), EXCLUSIVELY CHRISTIAN, BUT LARGELY UNKNOWN

You can judge the quality of their faith
from the way they behave.

Tertullian, "The Prescription against Heretics"

Although the concept of faith is sometimes used in a nonreligious sense, it is most frequently used as a religious concept, at least in English-speaking contexts. Used in the religious sense in countless books and articles, it is hardly ever formally defined, and when it is, those rare definitions are not consistent. In the religious sense, faith is largely perceived today as a subjective phenomenon that is not based on any historical facts or evidence. This nonevidential view of faith is the opposite of the faith of Christ's apostles and the early Christians in the New Testament, whose faith was linked to the historical authenticity of Christ's miracles, His crucifixion, and especially His bodily resurrection. These biblically historical events motivated His apostles to declare and present their eyewitness accounts orally and in writing to Christ's early followers. These accounts prompted and sustained the faith of Christians from the first century and to their descendants today.

Given this biblical background, this chapter serves as the standard-bearer of the New Testament's exclusively Christian concept of *pistis* (faith). Based on these biblical events, this faith played a significant role in the lives of the early Christians. That this faith in the New Testament pertained only to Christians is, however, a fact largely unknown by authors who over the years have written, or are writing, books and articles on this topic. Most Christians also do not realize that the faith of the early Christians in the New Testament is exclusively Christian, even many who have read and studied the entire New Testament. Thus, the following pages provide evidence to help overcome this long-existing, widespread void in biblical knowledge.

Faith (*Pistis*) Became a Religious Principle and Exclusively Christian

With the appearance of the New Testament, its writers innovatively took the Greek word *pistis* and used it as a religious principle and thereby also made it an exclusively Christian concept. This gave *pistis* a meaning and significance it previously did not have among the ancient Greeks. As William Henry Paine Hatch (1875–1972), America's renowned scholar of the Greek language, revealed in 1917, the Greek philosophy of Stoicism taught belief in supreme beings, "but of faith [*pistis*] as a principle of religion it made nothing."[3] Hatch further noted, "The fact is that faith was not an important factor in the religious life of the Stoics, and hence it

3 William Henry Paine Hatch, *The Pauline Idea of Faith in Its Relation to Jewish and Hellenistic Religion* (Cambridge, MA: Harvard University Press, 1917), 75.

played no conspicuous part in their religious teaching."[4] Similarly, Seneca (c. 4 BC–AD 65), Rome's stoical philosopher, taught that, in Roman thinking, the Latin concept of *fides* (faith) "belonged to the sphere of ethics rather than to that of religion."[5]

More recently, Dieter Lührmann (1939–2013), a German scholar of early Christianity, has shown that "'faith,' as a central category of Greek religious language, did not exist."[6] He also noted that "what is meant in early Christianity by 'faith' cannot be deduced by a general religious linguistic usage in the Hellenistic period."[7] And Teresa Morgan, a scholar of Early Church history at Oxford University, in her recent book *Roman Faith and Christian Faith* (2015), states that in the Greco-Roman world, "no one would begin a study of Greek or Roman religiosity by looking at *pistis/fides*; it does not play a large enough role in the evidence of any period."[8]

Faith (*pistis*) of the early Christians, in the words of Hatch, "was centered in Jesus Christ as Lord and Messiah, and it was primarily intellectual in character. But it also carried with it important ethical consequences, for it brought the believer into submission to the rule of Christ; and furthermore it formed the basis of the disciples' religious and social life."[9] Hatch further states that this "faith is from the beginning much more than belief or conviction, for it involved the feelings and the will as well as the intellect. Trust and

4 Ibid., 76.

5 Ibid.

6 Dieter Lührmann, "Faith," trans. Frank Witt Hughes, *Anchor Bible Dictionary*, eds. David Noel Freedman, Gary A. Herion, David F. Graf, John David Pleins (New York: Doubleday, 1992), 2:750.

7 Ibid.

8 Teresa Morgan, *Roman Faith and Christian Faith* (Oxford: Oxford University Press, 2015), 123.

9 Hatch, op. cit., 28.

loyalty are included in it."[10] Referring to the apostle Paul's use of faith, Hatch said, "Faith is the basic principle of Christianity and the distinguishing characteristic of Christians."[11] Similarly, Wilfred Cantwell Smith has stated that the New Testament "launched the concept [of] 'faith' in a big way, as virtually a distinctive Christian category."[12]

The religious meaning of faith and its exclusive role and nature in the New Testament is reflected by what the apostle Paul told the early Christians in Ephesus:

> For by grace you have been saved *through faith* [*dia pisteuos*]. And this is not of your own doing; it is the gift of God, not the result of works, so that no one may boast. For we are His workmanship, created in Christ Jesus for good works, which God prepared beforehand, that we should walk in them. (Ephesians 2:8–10, emphasis added)

Paul's portraying faith as "the gift of God" revealed its religious significance in that faith was not only the means to obtain eternal life but also the means to motivate Christ's followers to perform good works. As one observer has noted, faith to Paul was "not merely an intellectual assent to some proposition but a vital, personal commitment engaging the whole man . . . in all his relations with God, with other men, and with the world."[13]

10 Ibid., 35.

11 Ibid., 38.

12 Wilfred Cantwell Smith, *Belief and History* (Charlottesville: University Press of Virginia, 1977), 72.

13 Joseph A. Fitzmeyer, *The Jerome Biblical Commentary*, eds. Raymond E. Brown, Joseph A. Fitzmeyer, Roland E. Murphy (Englewood Cliffs, NJ: Prentice-Hall, 1968), 1:821.

Faith (*Pistis*), Its Christian Exclusiveness as a Mark of Identity

Teresa Morgan has recently stated that the "New Testament writers never use *pistis* language to refer to anyone other than Christians."[14] Similarly, Lührmann has shown that in the New Testament, "the Christian use of 'faith' is exclusive, and its object is God alone."[15] Lührmann has also revealed that Christianity made "frequent use of *pistis* to define itself," which is closely related to the exclusive nature of the Christian's use of faith.[16] The religious significance that the New Testament gave to *pistis* in the Greco-Roman world also functioned as an identity marker for the early followers of Jesus Christ. It distinguished them from non-Christians. Thus, in Acts 2:44, Luke refers to Christians as "the believing ones" (*oi pisteuontes*), and the apostle Paul in 2 Thessalonians 1:10 similarly writes "to the believers" (*tois pisteuousin*). These are only two examples of many in the New Testament which show that the designation of "the believing ones" referred only to Christians. It made them, according to Hatch, "a distinct social group, which was conscious of its separateness from the world and of its own solidarity, in which the obligations of brotherhood were vitalized and reinforced by a common principle of religion."[17] Thus, Gerhard Ebeling has stated, "There cannot be the least doubt that Christianity itself has at all times and in all places regarded *faith* as constituting its essence"[18] (emphasis added).

---

14 Morgan, op. cit., 235.

15 Lührmann, op. cit., 2:751.

16 Ibid., 2:752.

17 Hatch, op. cit., 51.

18 Gerhard Ebeling, *The Nature of Faith*, trans. Ronald Gregor Smith (Philadelphia: Muhlenberg Press, 1961), 20.

The New Testament speaks of only two kinds of people: (1) "the believing ones" (*oi pisteuontes*), those who had the exclusive faith, the Christians, and (2) those who were "the unbelieving ones" (*oi apistoi*), that is, those who had no faith. Hence, those with the exclusive *pistis* (faith) were identified as Christians in the pagan culture of the Greco-Roman world.

The Christians' Positive View of Faith (*Pistis*)

The Christian use of *pistis* also differed from the ancient Greeks' negative view of *pistis*. The Greeks saw *pistis* as "the lowest grade of cognition. It was the state of mind of the uneducated who believe[d] things on hearsay without being able to give reasons for their belief."[19] But contrary to the Greeks, the early Christians had a highly positive view of *pistis*. They even defended their *pistis* by pointing to factual, empirical evidence in support of it. This is evident in the words of the apostle Peter, who urged his fellow Christians to "always be ready to give a defense [*apologia*] to everyone who asks you a reason for the hope that is in you" (1 Peter 3:15 NKJV).

Peter was not the only one who urged the early Christians to defend their faith, prompted by the empirical event of Christ's bodily resurrection. Paul did so, too, when he told the skeptics in Corinth who doubted Christ's resurrection that not only had the risen Lord appeared to the apostles and to him personally, but He was also seen by more than five hundred other individuals, most of whom were still alive at the time of Paul's writing (see 1 Cor-

19 E. R. Dodds, *Pagan and Christian in an Age of Anxiety: Some Aspects of Religious Experience from Marcus Aurelius to Constantine* (Cambridge, UK: Cambridge University Press, 1965), 121.

inthians 15:4–8). Then, in the same chapter, Paul again defended the historical reality of Christ's bodily resurrection by telling the skeptics, "If Christ has not been raised, then our preaching is in vain and your faith is in vain" (1 Corinthians 15:14).

Paul also defended the faith of Christians, anchored in Christ's resurrection, when he boldly told the Greek philosophers, assembled on the Areopagus (Mars Hill) in Athens, that God had raised Christ from the dead (Acts 17:18–31). Another time, when standing as an accused victim before the skeptical King Agrippa, Paul told him that Christ's resurrection "was not done in a corner" (Acts 26:26 NKJV), indicating the resurrection was not an esoteric or hidden event but one known to the public at large. In short, Paul and the other apostles, unlike the Greeks, saw *pistis* not as the lowest grade of cognition but as a phenomenon based on evidence and thus worthy of sound, reasoned defense.

Luke, the apostle Paul's co-worker, similarly defended the validity of faith (*pistis*) when he reported that Jesus Christ had "presented Himself alive after His suffering by many *infallible proofs*, being seen by them during forty days and speaking of the things pertaining to the kingdom of God" (Acts 1:3 NKJV, emphasis added). Here it is important to note that the phrase "infallible proofs" in this citation is a translation of the Greek word *tekmeriois*, which Aristotle, the Greek philosopher, used in his book *Rhetoric I* to refer to irrefutable evidence.[20] This reference is compelling evidence that it was not the faith of Christ's apostles that prompted them to accept Christ's resurrection. Rather, it was Christ's postresurrection appear-

20 Aristotle, *The Art of Rhetoric* (Cambridge, MA: Harvard University Press, 1934), 27.

ances witnessed by the apostles during a period of forty days, along with having personally interacted with Him, that prompted and fortified their faith. These visible, empirical contacts made the historical reality of this event even more certain to them. Their accounts of Christ's resurrection were not the product of hearsay or mere faith, but in the words of the German exegete Karl Adam, "they had learned of His resurrection by way of sober sense perception, which is the only guarantee of genuine objective empirical knowledge."[21]

Another noteworthy defense of Christ's bodily resurrection was given by Luke when he wrote that "the apostles gave witness to the resurrection of the Lord Jesus" (Acts 4:33 NKJV). And when the apostles Peter and John were released from prison in Jerusalem and the authorities commanded them to cease talking about Christ's resurrection, what was their response? "We cannot but speak of what we have *seen* and *heard*" (Acts 4:20, emphases added). These affirmative words, well-known to the early Christians, assured them that their faith (*pistis*) was not the product of hearsay but the effect of sound, empirical evidence.

Similarly, it was the empirical evidence of Christ's risen body that dramatically produced faith in Thomas the apostle, who for an entire week had refused to accept the report from his fellow apostles who "told him" they had seen their risen Lord. And here it is important to note that the English translation, "the other disciples told him, 'We have seen the Lord'" (John 20:25), does not quite convey what the Greek verb *elegon* conveys. *Elegon*, an imperfect

21 Karl Adam, *The Christ of Faith: The Christology of the Church*, trans. Joyce Crick (New York: Pantheon Books, 1957), 350.

verb, indicates continuing action. Thus, it conveys more than the verb "told" in the past tense. This means the other disciples told Thomas several times in the one-week period they had seen the risen Lord. But he still refused to believe them.

Then one week later, when Christ again appeared to His disciples (including Thomas this time), Jesus asked Thomas to see and touch His crucifixion wounds. Upon seeing these wounds, Thomas declared, "My Lord and my God!" (John 20:28). It was Christ's bodily presence, together with the Holy Spirit present in Christ's words, that prompted Thomas's confession, a response of genuine faith, a faith he lacked before this empirical encounter. And it is noteworthy that the text does not say Thomas touched Christ's wounds. For him to see the wounds was enough.

Given that Acts 1:3 (noted above) states that Christ in His resurrected body showed Himself by "many infallible proofs" indicates His resurrection was not an imaginary event based on mere faith without evidence. To the contrary, His resurrection was an irrefutably empirical event, and His postresurrection appearances (of which about a dozen are mentioned in the New Testament) that occurred in a period of forty days, from the day of His resurrection to the day of His ascension to heaven, made His bodily resurrection even more convincing to those who saw Him after He had risen from the tomb.

The Exclusive Source of Faith

The early Christians' use of *pistis* (faith) was not only notably different from the Greeks' in terms of its religious significance. It also had a specific source: the Word of Jesus Christ, as Paul told the Christians in Rome. "So faith comes from hearing, and hearing through the word of Christ" (Romans 10:17). The early Christians heard the Word of Christ when His apostles in their preaching and writing assured them that they had personally seen Jesus Christ, the Word made flesh, before and after His resurrection appearances. Here the words of Peter are relevant: "This Jesus God raised up, and of that we all are witnesses" (Acts 2:32).

Moreover, if faith comes from hearing the Word of Christ, then the faith of Christians is God-derived. This truth further underscores the distinctive nature of their faith. Its Christ-centered source was another way that distinguished the Christians' use of *pistis/fides* from the pagan Greco-Romans. Hence, because the source of faith is Christ as the Word of God, it follows that anything called faith that does not come from that Word is not faith. As Jesus stated, "This is the work of God, that you *believe in* [*pisteunte eis*] Him whom He has sent" (John 6:29, emphasis added).

Alleged Faith of Non-Christian Religions

Space prevents me from showing how the faith of Christians differs from each of the world's many religions. However, it is not necessary to compare each of these religions' alleged faith with the New Testament's use of faith, for all non-Christian religions have one thing in common: their alleged faith is based on hearsay, non-eyewitness accounts.

The faith of Christians is based on, and prompted by, the eyewitness accounts of Christ's bodily resurrection reported by His apostles who had interacted with Him in person before and after His bodily resurrection. Then later, these same apostles signed their eyewitness testimony of Christ's resurrection in blood, so to speak, by unwaveringly adhering to their testimony even in the face of death, which all but one (the apostle John) eventually experienced as persecuted evangelists in different parts of the world. Here the words of Blaise Pascal (1623–62), the French philosopher-scientist, come to mind. Regarding the validity and authenticity of faith in Christianity's teachings, Pascal valued the eyewitness testimony that Christ's apostles gave pertaining to Christ's resurrection, and thus he said, "I believe only the histories of witnesses who get themselves killed."[22]

In contrast, consider the noneyewitness accounts for the alleged faith of Islam and Mormonism.

ISLAM

To Christians, faith is categorically different from what Muslims have been saying about faith since the seventh century, when Islam first appeared as a new religion. In about AD 610, Muhammad reportedly rushed home to tell his wife Khadija of an experience he had while resting in a cave at Mount Hira. He allegedly encountered an angel who told him to "recite," or read. While speaking to Khadija, he was greatly disturbed, saying that he was going mad. She consoled him, assuring him that he was not going mad, but that Allah had chosen him to be a prophet. Khadija's consoling words prompted him to accept her assurance of his san-

22 Blaise Pascal, *Pensees, Great Books of the Western World*, ed. Mortimer Adler (Chicago: Encyclopedia Britannica, Inc., 1996), 278.

ity and that he was indeed Allah's prophet. Thus, between AD 610 and 613 he began preaching in order to gain converts to his new religion. In his preaching, he claimed that Allah had made him a prophet (see Qur'an 19:30).

Interesting as this alleged account of Muhammad may be, it is important to underscore there is no eyewitness corroboration of what Muhammad allegedly had heard and later told Khadija about having had an angel (reportedly Gabriel) talk to him. In contrast, the accounts that the apostles of Jesus reported to others, and as recorded in the New Testament, about their having seen and interacted with the resurrected Christ were all based on their eyewitness accounts, courtroom-like evidence, not mere hearsay. Thus, lacking eyewitness accounts, the alleged faith of Muslims is based solely on hearsay.

Mormonism

Mormons honor Joseph Smith Jr. (1805–44) as their religion's founding prophet, based on his telling them he had received a divine revelation that appointed him to be their prophet. Over time, he gave several versions of this alleged revelation. In some versions, the location and his age differ. In another report, he saw an angel together with Jesus, and in still another version, God the Father and Jesus appeared to him. There are also differences regarding the instructions he received from the angel Moroni. The official Mormon version states that one evening in his bedroom the angel Moroni appeared to him in "a loose robe of the most exquisite whiteness."[23] Joseph said this happened the night of September 21,

23 See "Writings of Joseph Smith," *The Pearl of Great Price* (Salt Lake City: The Church of Jesus Christ of

1823, when he was seventeen years old. In this version, the angel Moroni told him there was "a book deposited, written upon golden plates, giving an account of former inhabitants of this [American] continent, and the source from whence they sprang."[24]

These plates were allegedly written by Mormon, the father of Moroni and an ancient prophet and commander-in-chief of a pre-Columbian people who reportedly once lived in America. Before the prophet Mormon died, he buried these plates in a hill of considerable size in western New York. Later, Moroni died and became the angel Moroni, who reportedly appeared to Smith on September 21, 1823, when Smith was told he would have to wait four years before he could access the plates. Four years later, on September 22, 1827, Smith allegedly obtained the plates, from which he then transcribed the Book of Mormon into English in 1830. From the angel Moroni's revelations, along with a special revelation transmitted to Smith—"thou shalt be called a seer, a translator, a prophet" (*Doctrine and Covenants* 21:1)[25]—he concluded that he was a prophet chosen by God to restore what he called "the great and abominable church, which is the whore of all the earth" (*Doctrine and Covenants* 29:21).

Joseph Smith's visions and what the angel Moroni allegedly said to him regarding the hidden plates are without a single eyewitness account, and thus his visions, like Muhammad's, are without any empirical verification. Hence, what Muslims and Mormons

---

Latter-day Saints, 1928), 50.

24 Ibid., 51.

25 *Doctrine and Covenants* contains revelations Mormons say Smith received from 1823 to 1843. It is one of today's official documents of the Church of Jesus Christ of Latter-day Saints.

call "faith" is merely blind faith in contrast to the faith of Christians, which is based on eyewitness evidence verified by Christ's martyred apostles.

Subjective and Objective Faith

Books, articles, newspaper reports, and informal conversations in the present day primarily speak of faith as referring to an individual or individuals subjectively believing something in the context of religion, often without an object. The New Testament, on the other hand, portrays faith as both subjective and objective. An example of subjective faith is when individuals accept Jesus Christ as their Lord and in Him have the assurance of justification and eternal salvation. This is expressed in the apostle Paul's words "If you confess with your mouth that Jesus is Lord and believe in your heart that God raised Him from the dead, you will be saved" (Romans 10:9). Another example of subjective faith is the response the frightened jailer at Philippi received when he asked, "Sirs, what must I do to be saved?" (Acts 16:30). Paul and Silas told him, "Believe in the Lord Jesus Christ, and you will be saved" (Acts 16:31). These references, as well as others in the New Testament, show that a Christian's subjective faith is anchored in Christ, the object of a Christian's faith.

The New Testament, however, also talks about faith in the objective sense, that is, the content of Christianity's teachings. For example, the apostle Paul predicted, "Some will depart from *the faith* (1 Timothy 4:1, emphasis added). Another example is Paul's saying, "The word of faith that we proclaim" (Romans 10:8).

The influential Church Father Augustine (AD 354–430) referred to objective faith in Latin as *fides quae creditur*, the faith that is believed. He called subjective faith *fides qua creditur*, the faith by which Christians believe. These two Latin concepts reveal another aspect of the exceptional nature of faith found in Christianity. Neither of these two Latin concepts would have made any sense to the Greco-Roman pagans because, as noted earlier, *pistis/fides* had no religious significance to them. Here it is also important to remember that paganism had no recorded creed or doctrine[26] and thus no objective content.

Regarding faith in the objective sense with reference to the Latin use of *fides*, American scholar Jaroslav Pelikan has noted that, in medieval usage, *fides* "must commonly be translated as 'the faith' rather than simply as 'faith,' because it referred in the first instance to the content of what was believed (*fides quae creditur*) rather than the act of believing (*fides qua creditur*), and specifically to one of the orthodox creeds of the church."[27] Pelikan added that, during the Protestant Reformation, "Luther's elevation of faith-as-trust over the Roman Catholic faith-as-credo still retained, and in some ways even intensified, the insistence on right doctrine, a knowledge of which and an assent to which were the necessary presupposition for a correct faith-as-trust."[28] Thus, Luther, like Paul, wanted Christians to know that objective faith is a vital component in the faith of Christians.

26 See Robin Lane Fox, *Pagans and Christians* (New York: Alfred Knopf, 1987), 31.

27 Jaroslav Pelikan, "Faith," *The Encyclopedia of Religion*, ed. Mircea Eliade (New York: Macmillan Publishing Company, 1987), 5:254

28 Ibid.

Since faith is today commonly seen as a subjective phenomenon, the objective aspect of faith (*fides quae creditur*) is thus largely unknown to many Christians when they think or talk about faith. This unfortunate reality prompted one modern theological observer to say, "Large sectors of contemporary Christianity are awash in a 'spirituality' of unbridled subjectivism."[29] This phenomenon is especially unfortunate because objective faith is a vital component of the exclusive faith of Christians.

Sola Fide (Faith Alone)

Martin Luther, who sparked the Protestant Reformation, tirelessly taught that Christians could obtain eternal life and salvation only through faith alone in Jesus Christ. He summed up this argument with the slogan of *sola fide*, "through faith alone." This slogan countered the Roman Church's doctrine, which taught that both faith and good works were necessary to obtain eternal life. Luther based his argument against that teaching on two Bible passages: (1) "For by grace you have been saved through faith. And this is not your own doing; it is the gift of God, not a result of works, so that no one may boast" (Ephesians 2:8–9), and (2) "For we hold that one is justified by faith apart from works of the law" (Romans 3:28). In conformity with these two passages that indicate what faith does, Luther defined *faith* this way:

> Faith is . . . a heartfelt confidence in God through Christ that Christ's suffering and death pertain to you

29 Richard John Neuhaus, "Theology for Church and Polis," in Carl E. Braaten and Philip Clayton, eds., *The Theology of Wolfhart Pannenberg* (Minneapolis: Augsburg Publishing House, 1988), 236.

> and should belong to you. . . . True faith . . . yields its whole heart to the conviction that the Son of God was given into death for us, that sin is remitted, that death is destroyed, and that these evils have been done away with—but, more than this, that eternal life, salvation, and glory, yes, God Himself have been restored to us, and that through the Son God has made us His children.[30]

The slogan of *sola fide* is an integral part of the New Testament's exclusive faith of Christians, the object of which is Jesus Christ and without whom there is no salvation, as He Himself has stated: "I am the way, and the truth, and the life. No one comes to the Father except through Me" (John 14:6).

Tripart Basis of the Exclusive Faith of Christians

Further exploring the *sola fide* concept, Luther's co-worker Philip Melanchthon defined *faith* as consisting of three parts, or elements: *notitia* (knowledge), *assensus* (assent), and *fiducia* (trust).[31] When Rome rejected this definition of faith, Melanchthon wrote the Apology of the Augsburg Confession to make it clear, lest people saw faith only as historical knowledge of Christ's death and resurrection, that Christians also needed personally to assent to and trust in Christ's redemptive work, "to want and to receive the offered promise of forgiveness of sins and of justification."[32]

30 Martin Luther, "Sermons on the Gospel of John," *Luther's Works* (St. Louis: Concordia Publishing House, 1957), 22:369.

31 See Philip Melanchthon, *Commonplaces:* Loci Communes *1521*, trans. Christian Preus (St. Louis: Concordia Publishing House, 2014), 119–21.

32 Ap IV 48.

The tripart definition of faith was not a novelty of Melanchthon at the time of the Reformation. In the seventeenth century, other theologians saw "*notitia* and *assensus* as preliminary steps to *fiducia*."[33] Nor did this definition first appear during the Reformation. According to Scottish theologian D. M. Baillie, this definition of faith goes back at least to "the Middle Ages, and perhaps further still."[34]

Occasionally, this classical definition of the faith still appears in a religious book or article. The periodical *Christianity Today* briefly discussed the three parts of faith in 1968 as one of several editorials.[35] For the most part, however, this definition is rarely found today, and thus many Christians do not know of this important definition of faith. Its rare appearance is apparently the product of today's nonevidential view of faith, also known as fideism.

It can be argued that this definition harks back to Christ's apostles. Their proclamations were based on their knowledge of Christ's physical resurrection, for they had seen Him in person on several occasions after He rose from the dead. They wanted their hearers to have faith in Christ's redemptive acts of salvation based on that historical knowledge, for their own faith was linked to this knowledge (*notitia*) to which they assented (*assensus*) and in which they trusted (*fiducia*).

This definition of faith sees knowledge as a necessary element in a Christian's faith. Similarly, Paul valued knowledge as part of

33 O. Kirn, "Faith," *The New Schaff-Herzog Encyclopedia of Religious Knowledge*, ed. Samuel Macauley Jackson (Grand Rapids: Baker Book House, 1950), 4:269.

34 D. M. Baillie, *Faith in God and Its Christian Consummation* (London: Faber and Faber, 1964), 108.

35 "Editorials: The Nature of Faith," *Christianity Today* (November 8, 1968), 34.

faith when he appealed to empirical knowledge by telling skeptics in Corinth that the resurrected Christ had "appeared to more than five hundred brothers at one time, most of whom are still alive" (1 Corinthians 15:6). As William Lane Craig has noted, "This reference shows that he [Paul] had personal knowledge of the people present at this appearance and that the appearance was not just a meaningless number on a list for him."[36] Craig adds, "One cannot dismiss this appearance as a mere legend, for Paul personally knew of people who had been at the appearance and could give first-hand testimony about it."[37]

The role of knowledge as a key component of faith was also the conviction of John Calvin (1509–64), the French-Genevan reformer. He stated, "Faith rests upon knowledge, not upon pious ignorance."[38] The tripart definition of faith did not lose its relevance after the Reformation. Three centuries later (in the 1850s), this definition was expounded in London by the renowned and highly esteemed preacher Charles Haddon Spurgeon (1834–92). In a sermon titled "Faith," he stated, "The first thing in faith is *knowledge*. A man cannot believe what he does not know. That is a clear self-evident axiom. If I have never heard of a thing in all my life, and do not know it, I cannot believe it."[39] He continued, "But a man may know a thing, and yet not have faith. I may know a thing, and yet not believe it. Therefore, *assent* must go with faith: that is to say,

---

36 William Lane Craig, *The Son Rises: The Historical Evidence for the Resurrection of Jesus* (Chicago: Moody Press, 1981), 94.

37 Ibid.

38 John Calvin, *Institutes of the Christian Religion*, ed. John T. McNeill, trans. Ford Lewis Battles (Philadelphia: The Westminster Press, 1960), 1:544.

39 C. H. Spurgeon, "Faith," *Sermons* (New York: Funk and Wagnalls Company, n.d.), 3:258.

what we know we must also agree unto, as being most certainly the verity of God."[40] And referring to the third part of faith, he asserted, "But man may have all this, and yet not possess true faith; for the chief part of faith lies in the last head, namely, in an *affiance* to the truth; not the believing it merely, but the taking hold of it as being ours, and in the resting on it for salvation."[41]

The tripart nature of faith, as the German theologian Wolfhart Pannenberg (1928–2014) has stated, was an important part of "classic Protestant dogmatics."[42] This fact, he insists, is important and relevant also in the twenty-first century. Thus, "knowledge of the ground of faith must, as such, logically precede faith."[43] This knowledge, he argues, finds its support in Romans 6:8–11, where the apostle Paul writes, "Now if we have died with Christ, we believe that we will also live with Him. We *know* that Christ, being raised from the dead, will never die again; death no longer has dominion over Him. For the death He died He died to sin, once for all, but the life He lives He lives to God. So you also must consider yourselves dead to sin and alive to God in Christ Jesus" (emphasis added).[44] Like Melanchthon, Pannenberg states that mere knowledge (*notitia*) of Christ's death and resurrection is not saving faith. Individuals, says he, must also give assent to this knowledge along with the trust that it has "a bearing on me" and is "for me."[45]

This biblically based tripart definition of faith is, however, no

40 Ibid., 259.

41 Ibid., 260.

42 Wolfhart Pannenberg, *Basic Questions in Theology* (Philadelphia: Fortress Press, 1971), 2:30.

43 Ibid., 32.

44 Ibid.

45 Ibid., 36.

longer accepted by many liberally minded Christians, largely as a result of the Enlightenment's rationalistic philosophy. Its proponents rejected many of the Bible's historically based accounts as historically unauthentic. This critical methodology is now the accepted method of biblical studies in departments of religion in many colleges and universities, as well as in many liberal Protestant and Roman Catholic theological seminaries. Bible critics have never been fond of knowledge (*notitia*) as a component in the definition of faith. Thus, faith is today commonly and erroneously viewed as independent of reliable knowledge and hijacked from the Bible's historical events, especially from Christ's miracles and His resurrection. (This higher-critical view is further discussed in chapter 2.)

Christ's Command to Proclaim the Exclusive Faith of Christians

Before Christ ascended to heaven, He told His disciples, "All authority in heaven and on earth has been given to Me. Go therefore and make disciples of all nations, baptizing them in the name of Father and of the Son and of the Holy Spirit, teaching them to observe all that I have commanded you" (Matthew 28:18–20). For centuries, Christians have referred to these words as the "Great Commission," which has had the effect of extending *fides quae creditur,* the faith that is believed.

The Great Commission commanded the disciples to make more disciples by baptizing and teaching them to observe Jesus' commands. This directive, of course, included the numerous teachings Christ had taught His disciples during the three years He had interacted with them. He had taught them to love God (Matthew

22:37), to love their enemies (Luke 6:35), to love their neighbors (Matthew 5:43), to love one another (John 13:34), to forgive one another (Matthew 6:15), to pray a prayer that He taught them (Luke 11:2–4), and to let their light shine by doing good works and thereby glorify their Father in heaven (Matthew 5:16).

When the disciple Thomas asked Jesus, "Lord, we do not know where You are going. How can we know the way?" (John 14:5), Jesus told him, "I am the way, and the truth, and the life. No one comes to the Father except through Me" (John 14:6). With this answer, Jesus taught Thomas and His other disciples that there was only one way to eternal life: faith in Him alone. In short, Jesus indicated that He was the sole object of their faith, and that was the message He wanted them to proclaim.

Peter later paraphrased these same words in his sermon on Pentecost Day, telling the early Christians, "And there is salvation in no one else [than Jesus], for there is no other name under heaven given among men by which we must be saved" (Acts 4:12). With these words, Peter underscored the value and significance of the distinctively exclusive faith of the Christians. Doing so, he revealed what some critics have called Christianity's "scandal of particularity," vis-à-vis other religions.[46] In a similar manner, Luke the evangelist called early Christianity "the Way,"[47] which revealed and encompassed its distinctive faith, as well as proclaiming that Christians were God's distinctive group.

---

46 Adolf Deissmann, "The Jesus of History," *Mysterium Christi: Christological Studies by British and German Theologians*, eds. G. K. H. Bell and Adolf Deissmann (London: Longmans, Green and Company, 1930), 31.

47 Referring to early Christianity as "the Way," the Book of Acts uses this appellation six times (Acts 9:2; 19:9, 23; 22:4; 24:14, 22).

Conclusion

Christianity has made numerous indelible imprints on the world.[48] When the New Testament writers took the Greek word *pistis* (faith) and used it as a religious principle by linking it to Jesus Christ and the biblical, historical phenomena of His miracles and His bodily resurrection, they made the faith of Christians an exclusive phenomenon. Yet for centuries, this exclusive nature of faith had apparently not been consciously perceived or noticed by Christian leaders in the post–New Testament era, even though many of the leaders had read, studied, and even preached on faith and its importance in the lives of their fellow Christians.

In part, the nonperception of this exclusive faith is understandable, for there is no declarative sentence in the New Testament that explicitly states that *pistis* and *pistis* language refer only to Christians. This characteristic of *pistis* (faith) is certainly there, but it must be consciously perceived, and for centuries Christian readers, including clergy and theologians, failed to do so. Had some writers of the New Testament explicitly stated that *pistis* (faith) is exclusively Christian, as Paul did regarding the exclusive nature of the Gospel by telling the Galatian Christians there is "not another" (Galatians 1:7 NKJV), the exclusive faith of Christians in the New Testament would likely not have remained unknown until the twentieth century. For as noted above, it was not until 1917 that William Henry Paine Hatch first revealed the important reality that faith in the New Testament is exclusively Christian. The reality of

48 For a detailed documentation of Christianity's many positive imprints, readers may wish to consult the volume by Alvin J. Schmidt, *How Christianity Has Changed the World* (Grand Rapids: Zondervan Publishing House, 2004).

this exclusive faith was further underscored by Dieter Lührmann in 1996 and then by Teresa Morgan in 2015.[49] Yet this important New Testament phenomenon continues to be largely unknown. This is evident when Christians so easily and unthinkingly ascribe faith to non-Christian religions by speaking of "the Islamic faith," "the Mormon faith," "the Buddhist faith," and so on.

In the next chapter, we will see how in the seventeenth and eighteenth centuries the European philosophy of the Enlightenment hijacked faith from its biblical, historical foundation when its proponents argued that faith needed no empirical or historical basis to be valid. This resulted in the nonevidential view of faith, now a common perception among critical scholars and many liberally minded Christians as well. Thus, "faith founded on fact," favorite words of John Warwick Montgomery,[50] is no longer acceptable to many who profess to be Christians.

Regarding Christ's physical resurrection that prompted and sustained the faith of His apostles, the early Christians, and the succeeding followers of Christ, numerous liberally minded clergy and similarly minded scholars are now teaching that Christ's resurrection has no reliable, historical foundation. With this stance, the exclusive faith of Christians was hijacked, which soon fostered various misuses of this Christ-centered concept. These misuses of faith are discussed and critiqued in the following chapters.

49 There may be some New Testament scholars other than the three cited here who have also noted the exclusively Christian role of *pistis* in the New Testament, but my research has not revealed any others.

50 See John Warwick Montgomery, *Faith Founded on Fact* (Nashville: Thomas Nelson, 1978).

DISCUSSION QUESTIONS

1. Why do you think the concept of faith is hardly ever formally defined?
2. What new meaning did the New Testament give to the Greek word *pistis* (faith) that was not true for the pagan Greeks?
3. How was the Roman concept of *fides* (faith) like *pistis* of the pagan Greeks?
4. What was distinctively different in the New Testament from the pagan Greeks regarding the use of *pistis* (faith)?
5. How did Christians in the New Testament, unlike the pagan Greeks, not see *pistis* (faith) as a negative concept?
6. Can you cite a reference from the New Testament that shows Christians had a positive view of *pistis* (faith)?
7. What does the Latin concept *fides quae creditur* mean?
8. How is *fides quae creditur* related to "objective faith"?
9. What does the Latin concept *fides qua creditur* mean?
10. How is *fides qua creditur* related to "subjective faith"?
11. Who in the New Testament is the exclusive source of *pistis* (faith)?
12. Compared to the New Testament, what do the teachings of all non-Christian religions lack regarding their foundation's authenticity?

CHAPTER 2

FAITH HIJACKED FROM ITS BIBLICAL, HISTORICAL FOUNDATION

> False words are not only evil . . . ,
> but they infect the soul with evil.
>
> *Socrates, in Plato's* Phaedo

From the Christian Church's earliest years, its laity, clergy, and theologians accepted the Law, the Prophets, and the Psalms of the Old Testament and the New Testament's canonical books as the revealed, inspired Word of God. These Scriptures included the four Gospels (Matthew, Mark, Luke, John), which report the accounts of Jesus' human and divine activities. The Church accepted His divine activities as authentic miracles that He in His supernatural power had performed, sometimes prompted by His compassion for people in need.

He turned water into wine at a wedding in Cana. He restored the sight of several blind men. He brought a widow's dead son back to life. He revived the dead daughter of a synagogue's ruler. He raised His dead friend Lazarus from the tomb. He cleansed ten men of leprosy. He healed a paralyzed man. He calmed a storm on the Sea of Galilee. He fed over five thousand people with two fish and five loaves. He healed a woman who had been crippled for eighteen years. He enabled people who could not hear or speak to do so. In addition to these miraculous acts, He rose bodily from the dead three days after He had been brutally and inhumanely crucified. The crucifixion and His bodily resurrection became the cornerstone, the foundation, and the pillar of the exclusive faith of Christians in the New Testament.

The Enlightenment's Radical View of Faith

Not long after Christ's ascension, some false teachers entered the Christian Church's fellowship, necessitating the convening of synods and councils to address the various issues and even emerging heresies. In time, the Church experienced two major schisms. The first schism occurred in 1054, when the Church in the East and the Church in the West formally severed their fellowship. The second major schism occurred with the Protestant Reformation in 1517. Despite these two significant schisms, the Church did not have any theologians who denied the historicity and the authenticity of Jesus Christ's miracles and His bodily resurrection.[51]

But when the Enlightenment (also called the Age of Reason) appeared in Europe in the seventeenth century and gained prominence in the eighteenth century, people began to question the historical veracity of Christ's miracles and His bodily resurrection. The core of Enlightenment philosophy is the superiority of rea-

51 Some may ask, "What about the Gnostics, who did not accept much of what the Early Church confessed and taught?" However, the Gnostics were never a formally recognized part of the Christian Church's fellowship.

son, which accepts what is recorded in the Bible only when it conforms with unmitigated human reason alone. This philosophical presupposition attracted numerous Bible critics. Soon these Bible critics denied the veracity of Christ's miracles, viewing them and His bodily resurrection as myths and legends. This philosophy led to their hijacking Christianity's concept of faith—that is, they took the established concept and began using it in a radically different manner from its past.

For the Bible critics, the historical foundation of the Bible was no longer necessary for faith to be valid. Faith became the mere pious concept of having faith in faith. Thus, for many theologians and laypeople today, *faith* no longer means what it meant in the New Testament and had meant for centuries in the Christian Church. Following is a brief overview of prominent Bible critics whose writings significantly contributed to the radical act of hijacking faith from its biblical, historical foundation.

Richard Simon (1638–1712), Early Bible Critic

A French Jesuit priest, Richard Simon was one of the first theologians to apply Enlightenment philosophy to Holy Scripture. In 1678, he published his book *Histoire critique du Vieux Testament* (A Critical History of the Old Testament). In 1682, this book was translated anonymously into English. Initially, some Roman Catholics saw his book as a useful aid to critique the Protestant Reformation's doctrine of *sola Scriptura*, which they disliked.[52] But Simon also argued that the Bible was only inspired in the passages

52 David Lyle Jeffrey and Gregory Maillet, *Christianity and Literature: Philosophical Foundations and Critical Practice* (Downers Grove: InterVarsity Press, 2011), 221.

that pertained to faith. Thus, he hijacked faith from the Bible's recorded historical events, arguing that the Pentateuch had inconsistencies and that Moses was likely not its only author. His critical approach applied to the Bible became known as "higher criticism" or the "historical-critical method," resulting in some historians calling Simon the father of higher criticism. This critical methodology soon attracted a growing number of liberally minded theologians, as well as many like-minded philosophers.

Before the historical-critical method of Richard Simon appeared, the faith of Christians and the faith of their pastors and theologians was based on the biblical, historical events of Christ's miracles, His crucifixion, and His bodily resurrection, as recorded in the New Testament. Christians knew that Christ's rising from the dead had conquered eternal death and damnation. Because of their Christ-centered faith, they looked forward to attaining Christ's promise of eternal life and joyfully recalled His words: "I am the resurrection and the life. Whoever believes in Me, though he die, yet shall he live, and everyone who lives and believes in Me shall never die" (John 11:25–26).

But the Enlightenment's Bible critics rejected Christianity's centuries-old doctrine of Christ's bodily resurrection as a historical phenomenon. They also rejected the authenticity of His miracles recorded in the four Gospels. Some considered the recorded miracles and His bodily resurrection as mere psychological projections of the apostles' subjective faith and their religious imagination, prompted by their great admiration of Jesus. The critics also denied the authenticity of all biblical revelation. Given their presupposition that the four Gospels and the epistles of the New Testament were not reliable, historical documents, they concluded the Bible was merely a book of faith. Thus, they hijacked faith from the Bible's historically reported events.

Gotthold Ephraim Lessing (1729–81) and His "Ugly Ditch"

Gotthold Lessing's father was a highly regarded, orthodox Lutheran pastor in Saxony who wanted Gotthold to study for the Lutheran ministry. But after a brief period of study, Lessing chose to become a devotee of the theater, a playwright, a free thinker, and an outspoken Bible critic. The latter was the product of his having adopted the Enlightenment's idol, the supremacy of reason. He gained notoriety after publishing parts of a lengthy manuscript, *An Apology for the Rational Reverers of God*. Though published anonymously, it contained highly provocative treatises written by Hermann Samuel Reimarus (1694–1768), a deist and professor of oriental languages at a secondary school in Hamburg, Germany, and an outspoken critic of the Bible.

Previously, Reimarus had never published any part of his manuscript in which he denied all biblical miracles, rejected divine revelation, and argued that Jesus had harbored messianic illusions. He also denied the historicity of Christ's resurrection and argued that His disciples were impostors who had stolen and hidden His crucified body. After Reimarus's death in 1768, his family gave the entire manuscript to Lessing. Lessing was the librarian in the town of Wolfenbuettel, and so the treatises became known as the *Wolfenbuettel Fragments*. As a free thinker, Lessing liked the radical content of the fragments and published them in 1774 without identifying their author. He titled the first fragment "On the Toleration of the Deists: Fragments of an Anonymous Writer."[53] The document argued that Jesus was a teacher of practical religion and that anyone who used reason and followed His teachings may call him- or herself a Christian. It also argued that Jesus' teachings had been corrupted by His apostles. It further contended that deists were to be tolerated, similar to the custom of tolerating Jews and pagans at the time when Reimarus wrote his fragments. However, the first fragment attracted little attention or pushback, so Lessing published five more fragments three years later.

The first of the five fragments asserted that only reason could prove the truth of the Christian religion, and thus clergy were advised not to disparage reason. The second fragment focused on the impossibility of biblical revelation, thus indicating it was incompatible with human reason. The third fragment questioned numerous details of Israel's exodus from Egypt to the Promised Land. The fourth fragment contended that the books of the Old Testament were not written to reveal a religion because they contained no doctrine pertaining to a future life or immortality of the soul. The fifth fragment, "On the Resurrection Narrative," highlights the differences and variations that the four Gospels report regarding Christ's resurrection and then concludes that Christ's bodily resurrection was therefore not a historical event.

Anticipating that the last fragment's heretical content would shock many biblically minded Christians, Lessing appended his

53 Henry Chadwick, trans., *Lessing's Theological Writings* (Stanford: Stanford University Press, 1957), 15.

"Editor's Counter-Propositions." It said objections could be raised regarding Reimarus's conclusions, and so, Lessing wrote,

> But how do this man's hypotheses, explanations, and proof affect the Christian? For him it is simply a fact—the Christianity which he feels to be true and in which he feels blessed. . . . In short, the letter is not the spirit, and the Bible is not religion. Consequently, objections to the letter and to the Bible are not also objections to the spirit and to religion.[54]

With these words, Lessing asserted that the validity of a Christian's faith does not depend on the objective facts of history. With this argument, he, like Simon, hijacked faith from the Bible's historical accounts. Thus, Christ's bodily resurrection that had been vouched for by Jesus' apostles as eyewitnesses, who testified they had personally seen and interacted with the resurrected Christ on several occasions, was rejected as a nonhistorical account. By hijacking faith from the historicity of Jesus Christ's resurrection, Lessing introduced the unbiblical view of faith that made it an act not based on historical evidence. This view of faith contradicts the exclusive faith of Christians based on the historical evidence of Christ's bodily resurrection. For the apostle Peter declared, "This Jesus God raised up, and of that we all are witnesses" (Acts 2:32). Similarly, Luke wrote to Theophilus, saying that Jesus had "presented Himself alive to them after His suffering by many proofs, appearing to them during forty days and speaking about the kingdom of God" (Acts 1:3). And the apostle Paul told skeptics in

54 Ibid., 17, 18.

Corinth that the resurrected Jesus had appeared to more than five hundred individuals at one time and that He had also appeared to James, the half-brother of Jesus, and to all the apostles, and finally to Paul himself (1 Corinthians 15:6–8).

The risen Christ also appeared to His apostles on several other occasions. At one of these appearances, He even ate some broiled fish with them (Luke 24:42–43). These face-to-face experiences with Him fortified and reinforced their faith in Him as their resurrected Lord and Savior.

Nevertheless, Lessing denied Christ's bodily resurrection, for the resurrection and Christ's miracles were what he called "accidental truths of history [that] can never become the proof of necessary truths of reason."[55] He called this difference an "ugly ditch" that in his mind he refused to cross. Unmitigated reason, not facts in history, was the sole and absolute determiner of truth for him.

Although Lessing grew up in a Lutheran parsonage with his father a Lutheran pastor, he rejected what Lutheran theology taught, consistent with Christian theology from at least since the Middle Ages, regarding the theological difference between ministerial and magisterial reason. Lutheran theology respects the use of ministerial reason in understanding biblical teachings. Ministerial reason functions as a servant that aids human understanding, for example, of biblical teachings, which sometimes may be above reason but not contrary to it. Magisterial reason, on other hand, rejects biblical teachings that it considers to be contrary to its norm of absolute, unmitigated reason as the only guide to truth.

55 Ibid., 53.

As one critic has noted, for Lessing, "the facts of history were in the nature of the case restricted by relativity and temporality, whereas the truths of reason were absolute and constant."[56] In other words, if Christian truth is historical, it cannot be absolute; or if it is absolute, it cannot be historical. Hence, Lessing rejected ministerial use of reason by subjecting everything in the Bible to magisterial reason. This method of reasoning also dominates the theological thinking of higher critics regarding their view of the Bible's content.

This meant that Lessing rejected the eyewitness accounts of Christ's apostles. To him, the apostles' accounts were merely reports of what they had seen with their eyes of faith, not reports of what happened in history. The apostles' faith was a faith without evidence. To Lessing, this kind of faith remained inviolate, even in the face of biblical criticism's heterodox conclusions; for him, the validity and benefit of Christ's resurrection for Christians do not depend on whether it happened in history, but whether Christians believe it happened. With this argument, Lessing saw Christians having faith in faith, which is blind credulity, better named *fideism*. This erroneous view of faith is discussed more fully in chapter 4, "From Faith to Fideism: A Deceptive Misuse of Faith."

David Friedrich Strauss (1808–74), an Unrepentant Apostate

Strauss grew up in Germany's region of Württemberg, and at age 17 he enrolled at Tübingen University, where he studied ancient

56 Philip Edgcumbe Hughes, "Reason, History, and Biblical Authenticity," *Christianity Today* (September 12, 1969), 3.

languages, philosophy, and theology. One biographer says that Strauss had already abandoned Christianity's biblically based doctrines by the time he graduated from the university in the summer of 1830, yet later he still agreed to serve a Lutheran congregation as curate (vicar). He conducted all parish duties, including preaching sermons, for nine months before leaving the congregation.[57]

In 1835, Strauss published *The Life of Jesus, Critically Examined.* It denied the miracles of Christ, His virgin birth, and His divine nature. He argued that the apostles' recorded accounts in the four Gospels that pertained to Christ's bodily resurrection were the product of their mythical imagination, rather than accounts of an empirical event that took place in history and of which they were eyewitnesses. The apostles' imagination was so powerful, said he, that it even moved them to see Jesus as the Messiah. Strauss denied the possibility that the supernatural was operative in the life of Jesus and in His performing miracles. In addition, he argued that the four Gospels could not be used to write a true biography of Jesus. Hence, as Horton Harris stated, "Strauss's *Life of Jesus* [book] was the most intellectually reasoned attack which had ever been mounted against Christianity."[58]

Despite Strauss's denial of biblical, historical Christianity, he still wrote the following: "The author is aware that the essence of the Christian faith is perfectly independent of his criticism."[59] By

---

57 David Friedrich Strauss, *The Christ of Faith and the Jesus of History: A Critique of Schleiermacher's Life of Jesus,* trans. and ed. Leander E. Keck (Philadelphia: Fortress Press, 1977), xxiii.

58 Horton Harris, *David Friedrich Strauss and His Theology* (Cambridge: At the University Press, 1973), 281–82.

59 David Friedrich Strauss, *The Life of Jesus, Critically Examined,* trans. and ed. Marian Evans (New York: Calvin Blanchard, 1860), 4.

this he meant that the key Christian teachings, such as Jesus' virgin birth, miracles, resurrection, and ascension, "remained eternal truths, although possessing no historical reality."[60] These teachings, he argued, were based on a Christian's faith, and thus they are not harmed or affected by historical critics denying their historical reality. As a theologian, Strauss knew that faith in God's saving grace, biblically speaking, is unequivocally linked to the empirical occurrence of Christ's resurrection. Strauss's denial of the resurrection then prompts an important question: Did he put forth this nonbiblical view of faith merely to prevent offending devout Christians who accepted the Bible's accounts as historically true and accurate?

The answer to this question may have been yes when he first published his book in 1835, but that answer would not have been true in his later life. For instance, in his final year, while terminally ill, he suffered great physical pain; he was not concerned about offending Christians—if he ever was—for he refused to read letters from Christians that urged him to repent and convert.[61] Nor did he find spiritual comfort in the words of Christ's Gospel. Instead, he enjoyed reading Plato's *Phaedo* in Greek. And consistent with his lack of faith and repentance, he gave uncommon, anti-Christian instructions to his children in his last will before his death on February 8, 1874.

He told them to make certain the Church would not be involved at his funeral, that there would be no church bells, no church music, no cross on the pall, no prayers, no speeches, and

60 Harris, op. cit., 52.

61 Strauss, op. cit., xlix.

no pastor present at the house or at the grave.[62] These instructions indicate that his hijacking of faith from its biblical, historical foundation clearly led to the destruction of the faith that he seemed to have had in his youth. His funeral instructions were the bitter fruit of his inveterate biblical criticism.

Martin Kähler (1835–1912), Proponent of Suprahistory

Kähler was the son of a Lutheran pastor, born the same year that David Friedrich Strauss published his heretical book *The Life of Jesus, Critically Examined*. Like other Bible critics, Kähler questioned the reliability of Christ's apostles' writings and argued that some of their accounts never happened in history. Like other critics of the Bible, he argued that a true biography of Jesus was not possible. Thus, he concluded, "We do not possess any sources for a life of Jesus which a historian can accept as reliable and sufficient."[63]

Some of Kähler's concepts have an aura of deception. For instance, when he spoke of the "historical Jesus," he did not mean Jesus as He is recorded in the four Gospels, but the Jesus who could be corroborated by historical-critical research. The name *Christ* did not mean the historical Jesus, but the Christ as proclaimed by His apostles' faith.[64] To Kähler, a Christian's faith was not based on Christ's bodily resurrection as an event that had happened in history. Rather, it was the Christian's faith experience prompted by the kerygma (the preached Christ) that made faith in the resurrection

62 Harris, op. cit., 257.

63 Martin Kähler, *Der sogenannte Jesus und der geschichtliche, biblische Christus* (Chr. Kaiser Verlag München, 1956), 21. Author's translation.

64 Emil Brunner, *Revelation and Reason: The Christian Doctrine of Faith and Knowledge*, trans. Olive Wyon (Philadelphia: The Westminster Press, 1946), 170.

theologically, though not historically, authentic: "The real Christ is the preached Christ whom Christians see with their eyes of faith."[65] In short, as George E. Ladd has noted, in Kähler's theology, "the risen Lord has no objective existence apart from the *kerygma*."[66] And as J. C. O'Neill has insightfully observed, "[Kähler] assumed that the body of Jesus that died was not raised from the dead. This follows from his assertion that the risen Christ is the preached Christ, and only the preached Christ; the resurrection marks the end of the historical Jesus."[67] In the theology of Kähler and other like-minded Bible critics, the "historical Jesus" was the term they used to refer to the Jesus who performed no miracles or any other supernatural acts.

The Bible critics' effort to distinguish between "the Christ of faith" and "the Christ of history" finds no support in the New Testament. This distinction is the product of the Enlightenment's presupposition that contends that miracles do not and never did happen. Thus, the kerygma concept was Kähler's deceitful way of teaching that Christ's bodily resurrection had not empirically occurred in history without clearly and honestly saying so to biblically minded laypeople. Kähler's concept of kerygma grossly ignores not only that the apostles wrote of Christ's miracles, crucifixion, bodily resurrection, and the salutary effects these events had in the lives and the faith of Christ's followers but also that they wrote to have them historically recorded for posterity. The apostles clearly

65 Kähler, op. cit., 44–45. Author's translation.

66 George E. Ladd, "Faith and History," *Bulletin of the Evangelical Theological Society* (1963), 91.

67 J. C. O'Neill, *The Bible's Authority: A Portrait Gallery of Thinkers from Lessing to Bultmann* (Edinburgh: T & T Clark, 1991), 172.

did not operate with Kähler's nonhistorical concept of the kerygma. For as the evangelist Luke assured the early Christians, it was "with great power the apostles gave witness to the resurrection of the Lord Jesus" (Acts 4:33 NKJV). Briefly put, the apostles saw their bodily resurrected Lord not with their eyes of faith but in person with their God-created physical eyes. This is what the kerygma concept denies, as it camouflages the denial of Christ's physical resurrection as an empirical event in history.

As Wolfhart Pannenberg has shown, in Kähler's theological concept of preaching Christ, "the real Jesus is not the picture of Jesus of Nazareth, but rather the Christ of faith who is experienced as a contemporary reality."[68] What was important to Kähler was not the historical Jesus as He really was, but the Jesus who provides existential meaning to those who hear Him declared in what Kähler called the kerygma.

Kähler distinguished events that occurred in history (*Historie*) from those that occurred in *Geschichte*, as he called it. The latter was the *übergeschichtlich* (suprahistorical) realm, where the suprahistorical Jesus performed His alleged miracles and where He rose from the dead. But historically speaking, Christ did not physically rise from the dead. Moreover, unlike the reported activities in the four Gospels, the events or activities that reportedly occurred in the realm of *Geschichte* cannot be examined by historians as to whether they are true or false. They can only be perceived as true in the eyes of a Christian's faith. Hence, Kähler's use of *Geschichte* in

68 Wolfhart Pannenberg, *Jesus—God and Man*, trans. Lewis L. Wilkins and Duane A. Priebe (Philadelphia: The Westminster Press, 1968), 25.

contrast to *Historie* is a subtle, deceptive way of hijacking faith from the historical events recorded in the New Testament. The concept of *Geschichte* separates faith from the "outward" facts of history to the individual's inward, subjective experience. In the words of J. C. O'Neill, this amounts to "a gigantic irrational faith in faith."[69]

Kähler presented himself as a Lutheran, but his kerygma concept, which does not accept the historicity of Christ's bodily resurrection, contradicts Lutheran theology as enunciated in the Book of Concord. This Lutheran document clearly upholds the historical resurrection of Jesus Christ. Moreover, in Kähler's kerygma, Jesus in the Gospels is not as He really was, for His apostles wrote about Him and His activities in the light of their subjective faith. Hence, the written words of Holy Scripture are not to be taken at face value, a conclusion that also spurns the Lutheran principle of *sola Scriptura*, which Martin Luther introduced several years before the Reformation's commonly cited date of 1517.[70] This doctrine was reaffirmed in the Lutheran Church's Epitome of the Formula of Concord of 1580, which states, "We believe, teach, and confess that the only rule and norm according to which all teachings, together with ‹all› teachers, should be evaluated and judged . . . are the prophetic and apostolic Scriptures of the Old and New Testament alone."[71] Finally, Kähler's concepts of *Geschichte* and *Historie* are also incompatible with Lutheran theology's teachings, given

69 O'Neill, op. cit., 178.

70 E. G. Schwiebert thinks Luther began to accept the doctrine of *sola Scriptura* in the first year of his teaching at the University of Wittenberg in 1508 to 1509. See Schwiebert's *Luther and His Times: The Reformation from a New Perspective* (St. Louis: Concordia Publishing House, 1950), 158.

71 FC Ep Summary 1.

that both concepts are contrary and foreign to the doctrine of Holy Scripture.

Paul Tillich (1886–1965), Faith as Ultimate Concern

Born in Germany, Tillich studied under Martin Kähler and was ordained as a Lutheran cleric. After he lost his teaching position in Germany in 1933 because of his anti-Nazi views, he spent most of his academic career in the United States, where he taught at Union Theological Seminary in New York, then at Harvard, and later at the University of Chicago.

Although of a Lutheran background, his theology had virtually nothing in common with the Lutheran Church's Book of Concord. He espoused the secular philosophy of existentialism, albeit with some Christian nuances. He also operated with the rationalistic presuppositions of the historical-critical methodology of biblical studies. Like other Bible critics, he saw faith as unrelated to the Bible's recorded historical events: "The truth of faith cannot be made dependent on the historical truth of the stories and legends in which faith has expressed itself. It is a disastrous distortion of the meaning of faith to identify it with belief in the historical validity of the biblical stories."[72] These words are the product of faith hijacked from its biblical, historical foundation.

Tillich's separating the concept of faith from history is the product of the higher-critical view of faith and history reminds one of N. T. Wright's criticism. He has rightly stated, "The idea that faith must never have anything to do with history, so popular

72 Paul Tillich, *Dynamics of Faith* (New York: Harper and Row, 1957), 87.

in certain circles for many years, is long overdue a decent burial."[73]

Tillich's theology reflects the philosophy of existentialism, which sees human existence in this world as essentially meaningless. According to Tillich, Christian existentialists see faith as a nonverifiable, existential concept in their quest for meaning in an absurd world. This view clashes with the faith of Christ's apostles, who upon having seen His miracles and His resurrected body confidently proclaimed in their eyewitness accounts the reality and the meaning of these events in the New Testament. This gave their existence meaning as they freely signed their eyewitness accounts in blood, so to speak, as persecuted martyrs in distant mission fields. They proclaimed these biblical, historical accounts with no nearby social support from their fellow apostles, for they were ministering and spreading the Gospel of their Lord in different parts of the then-known world, far removed from their fellow apostles, as they faithfully heeded Christ's Great Commission of Matthew 28:19–20.

Rudolf Bultmann (1884–1976)

The son of a Lutheran pastor and grandson of a Lutheran missionary, Rudolf Bultmann also studied to be a Lutheran pastor. But his theology, like Tillich's, was notably foreign to the Lutheran Book of Concord. He, too, saw himself as a Christian existentialist. In his position as a New Testament scholar, he gained notoriety by arguing, as did the apostate David Friedrich Strauss, that Christ's miracles recorded in the four Gospels never happened. Thus, they and other parts of the New Testament, in his opinion, needed to

73 N. T. Wright, *The Resurrection of the Son of God* (Minneapolis: Fortress Press, 2003), 716.

be demythologized. Christians in the twentieth century who lived with modern inventions such as radios, television, and moon rockets, Bultmann contended, cannot be expected to accept the historical veracity of the biblical miracles and especially not the miracle of Christ's bodily resurrection. Unfortunately, his quest to demythologize the New Testament, as George Florovsky has correctly noted, "de-historicizes Christianity."[74]

Influenced by Martin Kähler's concept of kerygmatic theology and his own existentialism, Bultmann argued it is not the historical Jesus that is important, but the Jesus who provides existential meaning for Christians when "the Christ of faith," not the Christ of history, is preached. In this way, Bultmann also hijacked the concept of faith from its foundation in Christ's miracles and bodily resurrection. Bultmann once declared, "Let it be most emphatically stated. It is of absolutely no importance for the Christian faith to prove the possibility or historicity of the miracles of Jesus as events of the past, but on the contrary, this would only be a confusion of the same."[75]

Karl Barth (1886–1968)

Born in Switzerland, Karl Barth hailed from a family of Calvinist clergy and spent most of his adult life as a professor of theology at several German universities. He is often seen as one of the most influential advocates of dialectical theology (frequently but incorrectly called neo-orthodoxy), a post–World War I phenomenon that subjects the Bible to the most radical form of historical criti-

74 George Florovsky, *Christianity and Culture* (Belmont, MA: Nordland Publishing Company, 1974), 32.

75 Rudolf Bultmann, "The Problem of Miracle," *Religion in Life* (Winter, 1957–58), 63–64.

cism but ironically still sees the Bible as a witness to the preached Word while rejecting the Bible as the Word of God itself.

In 1919, while still a parish pastor, Barth published *The Epistle to Romans*, which he revised in 1922. This work brought his theology to the fore by critiquing the liberal belief in the continued progress of the West's modern culture. Barth thought that World War I, with its countless tragedies, belied this liberal conviction. The Christian clergy in their preaching and teaching were not to identify with the modern culture's idea of progress but to preach God's revelation in Jesus Christ. Barth wanted Christianity not to become a product of culture, but ironically, he had accepted the historical-critical methodology, which was already a definite part of his European culture.

Barth produced numerous theological works, but most are verbose and inscrutable—his *Church Dogmatics* is nine thousand pages. In these works, he frequently uses the word *faith*, but it is never linked to the historicity of Christ's bodily resurrection, for to Barth, Christ's resurrection was not a historical event. He said, "We have already seen that the raising of Jesus from the dead is not an event in history elongated so as still to remain an event in the midst of other events." And he continued, "The Resurrection is the non-historical life of Jesus to its origin in God."[76] In short, like the other Bible critics, he hijacked faith from its biblical, historical foundation.

76 Karl Barth, *The Epistle of Romans*, trans. Edwyn C. Hoskins (London: Oxford University Press, 1933), 195.

Dietrich Bonhoeffer (1906–45)

To the general public, Dietrich Bonhoeffer is more widely known than the Bible critics discussed above, mostly because of the wide publicity he has received in numerous articles, books, and movies since World War II. The public outside of Germany first heard about him after the Nazi regime executed him on April 9, 1945, for his conspiratorial role in the July 20, 1944, assassination attempt on Adolf Hitler.

Since that tragic event, Bonhoeffer has been admired by groups with notably disparate convictions. For example, many conservative and evangelical Christians and numerous liberally minded Christians tend to see him as one who lived an evangelically based Christian life. Thus, in the words of Richard Weikart, Bonhoeffer became "a mythic hero in the pantheon of late twentieth-century Christianity."[77]

There appear to be two reasons why many Christians hold a highly favorable view of Bonhoeffer. One stems from their having heard the laudatory publicity he has received in articles, books, videos, and movies. The other seems to lie in their likely having only read one or two of his most widely cited books, *The Cost of Discipleship* (1937) and *Life Together* (1939). Both books accent the importance of living devoutly, heeding biblical teachings, and reading the Holy Scriptures. Neither of these two books reveals the skeptical views he expressed in other publications. Weikart says these two books have been the "favorite books in evangelical circles."[78]

---

77 Richard Weikart, "Scripture and Myth in Dietrich Bonhoeffer," *Fides et Historia* (1993), 12.

78 Ibid., 13.

Not commonly known to the conservative and evangelical admirers of Bonhoeffer are the praises he has received from supporters of the higher-critical method of biblical studies for his arguing that the Bible contains legends and myths. He has even received praises from the advocates of the God-is-dead movement. Some of the latter proponents have even "appealed to him as a forerunner of their theology."[79]

Thus, it appears the praises Bonhoeffer has received from so many Christians are likely the result of their not having read or heard of his biblically critical pronouncements that pertain to some core biblical teachings, such as his contending that Christ's resurrection did not occur in history but "in the sphere of faith" (*in der Sphäre des Glaubens*).[80] He said that for Christians to see Christ's resurrection as a historical phenomenon was "senseless and crude" (*sinnlos und grob*),[81] and he asserted that "history provides no absolute foundation for faith" (*Von der Historie aus gibt es keinen absolute Grund des Glaubens*).[82] Thus, like other Bible critics, he hijacked the faith from its biblical, historical foundation.

Interestingly, regarding Bultmann's demythologizing of the New Testament (noted above), Bonhoeffer disagreed with those who criticized Bultmann for having gone "too far" (*zu weit*) in demythologizing Scripture. Instead, Bonhoeffer argued that Bultmann had "not gone far enough" (*sondern zu wenig weit gegan-*

79 Richard Weikart, "So Many Different Dietrich Bonhoeffers," *Trinity Journal 32NS* (2011), 71.

80 Dietrich Bonhoeffer, *Jugend und Studium*, 1918–27 (Munich: Chr. Kaiser Verlag, 1986), 319.

81 Ibid.

82 Dietrich Bonhoeffer, *Wer Ist und War Jesus Christus?* (Hamburg: Furche-Verlag, 1962), 65.

gen ist).[83] Here it seems appropriate to note that Bonhoeffer, like Kähler, also identified himself as Lutheran, even though he, too, rejected the Lutheran Church's Book of Concord's stalwart affirmations of the historicity of Christ's bodily resurrection.

Like David Friedrich Strauss and Martin Kähler, Bonhoeffer said, "The life of Jesus cannot be written" (*Vita Jesu scribi non potest*).[84] Why not? Because, in his opinion, too many myths and legends had arisen regarding Jesus' life. This radical stance is another example that is not known to many Christian admirers of Bonhoeffer.

Conclusion

The devastating harm the above Bible critics have done to biblical Christianity by hijacking its exclusive faith from its biblical, historical foundation of Christ's miracles and His bodily resurrection is one of the most tragic heresies tolerated and taught in many liberal churches today. These critics, and others like them, who accept the hijacking of faith from its biblical, historical foundation have failed to tell the Christian public in plain and simple language that this act of theirs has made faith akin to faith in faith, better known as blind faith or fideism. Thus, the words of Wilfried Joest, an advocate of liberal or dialectic theology, seem appropriate here. According to him, faith is "an intangible and supersensory event which cannot be described in psychological terms; it is a

83 Dietrich Bonhoeffer, *Widerstand und Ergebung: Briefe und Aufzeichnungen aus der Haft* (Munich: Chr. Kaiser Verlag, 1952), 183.

84 Dietrich Bonhoeffer, *Gesammelte Schriften* (Munich: Chr. Kaiser Verlag, 1972), 5:138.

'vacuum.'"[85] Not to be impolite, but one must ask, how does Joest's concept of faith differ from an eight-year-old child having faith in the proverbial tooth fairy? In short, the faith espoused in liberal theology is not the faith found in the New Testament.

Equally tragic is the undeniable truth that similar antibiblical, subjective views of faith are now held by numerous individuals, largely because they have not learned or have not accepted that faith, according to the New Testament, is linked to the "foundation of the apostles and prophets, Jesus Christ Himself being the chief cornerstone" (Ephesians 2:20). For it was Jesus Christ and His bodily resurrection, a historical event, that prompted the faith of the early Christians, who by God's grace were assured of the forgiveness of their sins, justification, and the promise of eternal life.

But once the exclusive faith of Christianity was hijacked from its biblical, historical foundation, faith could be ascribed to any religion. That effort is alive and active in today's synonymizing of *faith* and *religion*, a common phenomenon discussed in the next chapter.

---

85 Wilfried Joest, "Dialectic Theology," *The Encyclopedia of the Lutheran Church*, ed. Julius Bodensieck (Minneapolis: Augsburg Publishing House, 1965), 698.

DISCUSSION QUESTIONS

1. Why is the Enlightenment also known as the Age of Reason?
2. How do Bible critics view biblical revelation?
3. How does the Bible critics' concept of faith depart from the biblical concept of faith?
4. How does ministerial reason differ from magisterial reason?
5. David Friedrich Strauss said biblical criticism does not negatively affect the validity of faith. Show how he personally did not believe this argument.
6. In liberal theology, how is "the Christ of history" not the same as "the Christ of faith"?
7. What do Bible critics mean by "the historical Jesus"?
8. How does Martin Kähler's kerygma (preaching Christ) deceptively deny Christ's bodily resurrection as a historical event?
9. What does demythologizing the New Testament mean, according to Rudolf Bultmann?
10. What did Dietrich Bonhoeffer say about the historicity of Christ's bodily resurrection?
11. What did Bonhoeffer say about Bultmann's demythologizing the Bible?
12. Why do many Bible critics say a biography of Jesus cannot be written?

CHAPTER 3

FAITH AND *RELIGION* SYNONYMIZED, TODAY'S POPULAR MISUSE OF FAITH

Many false prophets will arise and lead many astray.

Jesus Christ (Matthew 24:11)

The exclusive faith of Christians, unequivocally taught in the New Testament, has now essentially lost its exclusive meaning, not only because it has been removed from its biblical, historical foundation, but also because the word *faith* has been made a synonym for *religion*. The synonymizing of *faith* and *religion* equates faith with religion—any religion. This faulty equation is now widely accepted in the English-speaking world. When newspapers, scholarly journals, and books write about faith and religion, they invariably use these two words interchangeably. This practice is now so common that numerous devout, undiscerning Christians also use these two concepts as synonyms. They fail to realize that synonymizing *faith* and *religion* contradicts Christianity's exclusive faith as consistently portrayed in the New Testament.

How and When *Faith* and *Religion* Became Synonyms

For nearly two millennia, Christianity's concept of *pistis* (faith) revolved around and focused on the historical events of Christ's miracles, His crucifixion, and His bodily resurrection, as reported by the apostles' eyewitness accounts in the New Testament. But with the advent of the Enlightenment, the Bible critics hijacked the faith of Christians from these events by questioning the veracity of Christ's miracles and His resurrection, which had prompted and sustained the faith of the early Christians.

The Enlightenment era opened the door for Bible critics to argue that members of non-Christian religions also had faith, even though those religions had never claimed to have faith based on historical miracles verified by eyewitness accounts like those of Christ's apostles. The theologian and Bible critic who first ascribed faith to all religions was the German theologian Friedrich Schleiermacher, who became popular in radically oriented theological circles in Berlin beginning in 1810. A decade later, he published his book *Der christliche Glaube nach den Grundsätzen der evangelischen Kirche in Zusammenhange dargestellt* (later translated into English with a shorter title, *The Christian Faith*) in which he took the radical step of synonymizing *faith* and *religion*.

Along with synonymizing *faith* and *religion*, Schleiermacher referred to non-Christian religions as "*andern Glaubensweisen*" (other faiths), rather than "*andern Religionen*" (other religions). According to Wilfred Cantwell Smith, Schleiermacher was "the first thinker in history to write a theology explicitly considering the

Christian as one among several modes of faith (*Glaubensweisen*, as he dynamically worded it)."[86] With this newly coined word, Schleiermacher ascribed faith to non-Christian religions, thus indicating that for him *pistis* (faith) was not Christianity's exclusive concept as taught in the New Testament. Furthermore, his use of *Glaubensweisen* (faiths) was not derived from any ancient Greek literature, where *pisteis*, the plural of *pistis*, never meant "faiths" in the Greek culture. In Aristotle's *Rhetoric*, for example, the concept of *pisteis* pertains to "modes of persuasion, or rhetorical proof."[87] It referred to persuasive communication. Thus, the plural *Glaubensweisen* (faiths) was a syncretistic neologism with no relationship to the history, grammar, or syntax of ancient Greek.

The Plural of *Pistis* (*Pisteis)* Not in the New Testament

While the ancient Greek language does indeed have the word *pisteis*, the plural of *pistis*, this plural word does not appear in the New Testament. As Andrew Shanks has recently shown, "To designate the most significant sort of truth, [the apostle Paul] chose a word [*pistis*] that, in the relevant sense, functioned only in the singular."[88] That "significant sort of truth," as Paul's epistles show, is the content of Christ's redemptive work, accomplished by His crucifixion and bodily resurrection. In short, it is *pistis* in the singular, not *pisteis* in the plural, that is unique and exclusive in the New Testament.

---

86 Wilfred Cantwell Smith, "On Mistranslations of Book Titles," *Religious Studies* (March 1984), 36.

87 *The Rhetoric of Aristotle with a Commentary*, Edward Meredith Cope and John Edwin Sandys, eds. (Cambridge, UK: Cambridge University Press, 1877), 196.

88 Andrew Shanks, *Hegel versus Inter-Faith Dialogue: A General Theory of True Xenophilia* (New York: Cambridge University Press, 2015), 17.

Shanks further states that in Paul's writings, "the oneness of true Faith [*sic*] surely corresponds, in the most direct fashion, to the oneness of God."[89] He also contends that "to accord excessive theological significance to the difference between 'faiths' in the plural is, by contrast, to be trapped in the sort of trivializing delusion that comes to its most overt expression in polytheistic form."[90] In other words, when individuals speak of religions as "faiths," they "have not really grasped the proper point of monotheism."[91] In short, they are more in tune with polytheism than with monotheism. This is a strong indictment by Shanks of those who today speak of "faiths" instead of "religions," which is a part of the "interfaith" mindset of today's English-speaking populace. Shanks calls today's interfaith mentality "a wretched notion."[92] His observation is revealing, given that so many Christians today seem not to realize that interfaith values undermine the exclusive faith of Christians found in the New Testament. As writer Mollie Ziegler has aptly stated, "Interfaith is no faith."[93]

Schleiermacher's pluralizing *faith* and synonymizing *faith* and *religion*, contrary to the New Testament's exclusive Christian use of *faith*, apparently posed no problem for him. There is no evidence he had ever accepted the New Testament's portrayal of faith as exclusively Christian or the classic definition of faith as consisting

89 Ibid.

90 Ibid.

91 Ibid.

92 Ibid., 1.

93 Mollie Ziegler, "Interfaith Is No Faith," *Wall Street Journal* (July 19, 2002), W15.

of *notitia* (knowledge), *assensus* (assent), and *fiducia* (trust).[94] His two radical moves reflected his apostasy, a stance he had already assumed at the early age of nineteen when he wrote to his father, a Reformed chaplain in the Prussian army. In the letter, he confessed:

> Faith is the regalia of the Godhead, you say. Alas, dearest father, if you believe that without this faith no one can attain salvation in the next world, nor to tranquility in this—and such, I know is your belief—oh, then pray to God to grant it to me, for to me it is now lost. I cannot believe that he who called himself the Son of Man was the true, eternal God. I cannot believe that his death was a vicarious atonement.[95]

Thus, he denied the New Testament's exclusive faith of Christians that included all these biblical doctrines that he spurned. They clashed with his syncretistic efforts of ascribing faith to all religions by calling them "*Glaubensweisen*" (faiths).

Faith in Titles of Books and Articles

The synonymizing of *faith* and *religion* has resulted in the concept of faith preempting the concept of religion. This practice in English is now common in titles of books, articles, speeches, and sermons, even when it is not faith but religion that is discussed. Below I cite two books and one article to illustrate this current practice, where three titles use the word *faith*, but the word *religion* in

94 I refer to the definition of faith as *notitia*, *assensus*, and *fiducia* as classic given that D. M. Baillie in his *Faith in God and Its Consummation: The Kerr Lectures for 1926* (Edinburgh: T and T Clark, 1927), 108, shows that this definition reaches back to the early Middle Ages.

95 Brian Albert Gerrish, *A Prince of the Church: Schleiermacher and the Beginnings of Modern Theology* (Philadelphia: Fortress Press, 1984), 25.

each case would have been the correct choice.

The Faith of Japan by Tasuku Harada (1914) is one of the early books published a century ago that used the word *faith* instead of *religion* in its title. This volume consists of Donald B. MacDonald's "The Hartford-Lamson Lectures on the Religions of the World" (1909). These lectures discuss Japan's religions of Tao and Zen Buddhism's concept of Satori, along with Shintoism's Kami and Michi. The author and publisher selected *faith* as the title's keyword, ignoring the lectures in this book that used the word *religions*, not *faiths*. A far better and more accurate title would have been *The Religions of Japan*.

The relatively recent book *Faith-Based Diplomacy: Trumping Realpolitik* (2003) by Douglas Johnston discusses the religious teachings of Buddhism, Judaism, and Islam and some Christian principles. The book consistently mentions religion, not faith. But the author and the publisher, in tune with today's cultural preference for the word *faith*, chose *faith* instead.

The article "The Marketplace of Faith," published in the *Wall Street Journal* (December 28, 2018), is an opinion piece of about twelve hundred words. It contains the word *faith*, but the article has nothing to do with faith. It discusses the relationship between economics and religion—not faith. The words *religion* and *religious* appear thirty-four times, and *faith* appears only twice. Hence, the word *religion* would have been far more appropriate in the title of this article.

The Singular *Faith* in Phrases

Declaring *faith* and *religion* as synonyms has, especially in recent years, evolved into numerous phrases using *faith* in the singular, now found in countless books, articles, and speeches. The following phrases have appeared in various religious and secular publications: "people of faith," "person of faith," "women of faith," "legacy of faith," "new faith," "contours of faith," "faith event," "faith journey," "faith-based fraud," "faith-based programs," "leap of faith," "faith crimes," "violent faith," "murderous faith," "faith friendly," "shape of faith," "streams of faith," "global rise of faith," "faith vocabulary," "interfaith," "non-Christian faith," "fleeing faith," "why faith endures," "triumph of faith," "faith community," "faith-affiliated schools," "faith-driven," "faith-formed," "faith leaders," "faith traditions," "faith politics," and "faith leaders," and one publication even wrote about "Voodoo faith."

Of these faith phrases, "people of faith," which refers to individuals with religious convictions from a variety of religions, is now frequently heard in speeches and seen in print. Sometimes this phrase is also heard in political speeches. "People of faith" is not associated with any specific religious identity, which makes it an acceptable part of today's efforts to promote multiculturalism, a phenomenon that became increasingly more common in English-speaking countries since the 1990s. As these countries have continued promoting multiculturalism, the phrase "people of faith"[96] now appears in countless books, articles, and speeches.

96 Twenty years before the phrase "people of faith" became popular in American culture in the 1990s, an English translation of Martin Luther's Latin "Lectures on Romans" (compiled in 1515) appeared in *Luther's Works*, translated by J. A. O. Preus, ed., Hilton C. Oswald (St. Louis: Concordia Publishing

One cannot help but ask, what do these faith phrases—such as "contours of faith," "faith journey," and "shape of faith"—really mean? Why do editors of books and articles accept these faith phrases? The phrases appear to be mere buzzwords that provide no meaningful information.

Faiths in Titles of Books and Articles

Some fifty years after *faith* was pluralized in the 1820s in German with the word *Glaubensweisen* (faiths), this new concept made its way to England. In 1873, Thomas Inman, a British physician and Bible critic, published his book *Ancient Faiths Embodied in Ancient Time.* Two decades later, in 1891, John M. Mitchell and Sir William Muir also used the word *faiths* in their jointly authored book's title, *Two Old Faiths: Essays on the Religions of the Hindus and the Mohammedans.*

The use of *faiths* in titles of books and articles became more common in the 1900s, especially following World War I (1914–18). By the mid to the latter part of the 1900s, and during the first two decades of the twenty-first century, an increasing number of authors wrote of religions as "faiths" in book titles and their content.

Despite the growing frequency of the word *faiths* appearing in books and articles, there still were notable authors who did not adopt this new word as a synonym for *religions*. The well-known British historian Arnold Toynbee titled his book *An Historical Ap-*

House, 1972), 25:252. This Latin document contains the following sentence: "*Populus itaque fide totam vitam suam agit in querendo Iustifcationem.*" Preus translated this sentence as "the *people of faith* spend their whole life seeking justification" (emphasis added). I cite this as an interesting coincidental example that contains the phrase "people of faith" nearly five hundred years before this same phrase became popular in English in the 1990s. I know of no evidence, however, that the translation by Preus in 1972 gave rise to the current phrase "people of faith" some twenty years later.

proach to Religion in 1956. The book did not have *faith* or *faiths* in its title. Similarly, C. S. Lewis did not use *faiths* in his illuminating book *Surprised by Joy: The Shape of My Early Life* (1955), in which he wrote about "the perplexing multiplicity of religions," rather than the "multiplicity of faiths." Nor did Will Herberg, an American scholar, see *faith* and *religion* as synonyms in his book *Protestant, Catholic, Jew: An Essay in American Religious Sociology* (1960). He wrote about "religion in America," not about "faith in America." Thus, when we look at recent books in print, we still find numerous books that focus on religion that do not see *faith* or *faiths* replacing the word *religion* or *religions*, either in their titles or in their discussions and analyses.

The Plural *Faiths* in Phrases

The plural word *faiths* is now an integral part of the English language, even though there is not the remotest hint of the plural in the New Testament. When authors or speakers speak of "faiths," they lack a biblical basis for its use because, as noted earlier, *pistis* (faith) never appears as plural in the New Testament.

Along with the word *faiths* in place of *religions* in titles of books and articles, we also find all sorts of *faiths* phrases dotting their pages. The following are some current examples: "Asian faiths," "African faiths," "Eastern faiths," "Western faiths," "diverse faiths," "great faiths," "violent faiths," "all faiths," "many faiths," "no faiths," "unchurched faiths," "low-tension faiths," "high-tension faiths," "other faiths," "permissive faiths," "world faiths," "organized faiths," "homegrown faiths," "foreign faiths," "multiple faiths," "community faiths," "different faiths," "competing faiths," "homogeneous faiths," "heterogeneous faiths," "non-Christian faiths," and the oxymoronic "godless faiths." Some of these phrases are of relatively recent origin.

Faith and *Religion* Synonymized Clashes with Christ's Teachings

Following the synonymizing of *faith* and *religion*, all religious teachings, especially with the West's recent acceptance of multiculturalism, essentially came to be viewed as having equal truth value. The teachings of Christianity, Islam, Buddhism, Hinduism, Jainism, and all other religions, regardless of the glaring contradictions that exist between any two or more religions, are accepted as equally true, beneficial, and valid "faiths." But given the West's current adherence to multiculturalism, these contradictions are not recognized. Thus, it seems appropriate to cite only a few examples that clash with Christ's teachings.

Jesus taught, "You shall love your neighbor as yourself" (Matthew 19:19), but Muhammad taught in the Qur'an that Muslims cannot have Jews or Christians as friends (Qur'an 5:51). Another time, Jesus stated, "You shall worship the Lord your God, and Him only shall you serve" (Luke 4:8), but Hinduism teaches there are forty-two gods and goddesses. Jesus also taught that eternal life could be attained only through faith in Him: "I am the way, and the truth, and the life. No one comes to the Father except through Me" (John 14:6); but Jainism and Buddhism, for example, teach that nirvana can be attained without Christ. Additional contradictions vis-à-vis Christ's teachings and those of non-Christian religions are numerous.

Today's widespread ignoring of these contradictions in the name of "toleration" merits citing a pertinent, insightful critique voiced by the renowned American sociologist Peter L. Berger. Cogently, he once wrote, "If I propose that all religious traditions are equal in their truth contents, I am saying in effect that there is no such thing as truth."[97] He, of course, is right. But given today's penchant for political correctness in the West, Berger's logical comment falls on deaf ears.

Contrary to the West now accepting the teachings and practices of all religions as having equal truth value, Jesus taught that only those who had faith in Him had authentic, saving faith. Speaking of Himself, Jesus told Nicodemus, a Pharisee and a member of the Jewish Sanhedrin, "Whoever believes in Him is not condemned, but whoever does not believe is condemned already, because he has not believed in the name of the only Son of God" (John 3:18).

Jesus Spoke of Only One Faith, Not Many "Faiths"

Speaking about the end of time, Jesus once lamentingly asked, "When the Son of Man comes, will He find faith on earth?" (Luke 18:8). Here it is important to note that the Greek text does not simply say "faith," as most translations render this reference. Rather it says, "the faith" (*ten pistin*), that is, the exclusive faith of Christians, the faith that has Christ and His teachings as the object of their faith. Jesus did not ask whether He, the Son of Man, would find "faiths" on earth. His saying "the faith" indicates that today's pluralizing of *faith* as *faiths* is a heresy, now ironically, though likely unwittingly, often uttered even by Christians.

97 Peter L. Berger, *A Far Glory: The Quest for Faith in an Age of Credulity* (New York: The Free Press, 1992), 153.

"One Lord, One Faith, One Baptism"

The syncretistic use of *faith* as a synonym for *religion* or *faiths* for *religions* clearly clashes with the apostle Paul's comforting words he penned to the early Christians in Ephesus when he assured them that there was only "one Lord, *one faith*, one baptism" (Ephesians 4:5, emphasis added). In short, Paul did not say there was another "faith" (*pistis*) or religion available in God's plan of salvation. Thus, when devout, committed Christians today, influenced by their culture, speak or write using the syncretistic concept of "faiths" when referring to other religions, they are saying, likely unwittingly, that the faith of Christians as taught in the New Testament is not exclusive and that faith is also an important principle in non-Christian religions.

Faith and *Religion* as Synonyms Makes Christianity Just Another Religion

Thus far I have used the phrase "non-Christian religion," which implies that Christianity is also a religion. While we today may refer to Christianity as a religion, biblically speaking, it is also more than just a religion. Here it is important to consider this observation by British theologian N. T. Wright: "When Christianity is made 'just a religion,' it first muzzles and then silences altogether the message the gospels were eager to get across."[98] He continues, "When that happens, the gospel message is substantially neutralized as a force in the world beyond the realm of private spirituality

98 N. T. Wright, *How God Became King: The Forgotten Story of the Gospels* (New York: Harper One, 2012), 164.

and an escapist heaven."[99] Given this phenomenon, Wright critically adds, "And the churches have, by and large, gone along for the ride."[100]

Indeed, Christianity is more than just a religion. Christ, through His suffering, death, and bodily resurrection, not only obtained eternal salvation for all who in faith confess Him as their Lord, but He also wants His followers to "let your light shine before others, so that they may see your good works and give glory to your Father who is in heaven" (Matthew 5:16). Certainly, Christians are justified by grace through faith in Christ, as Paul wrote: "For by grace you have been saved through faith. And this is not your own doing; it is the gift of God, not a result of works, so that no one may boast" (Ephesians 2:8–9). But they are not saved only for eternal life, for in the next verse, Paul told the Ephesian Christians, "For we are His workmanship, created in Christ Jesus for good works, which God prepared beforehand, that we should walk in them" (Ephesians 2:10). Hence, Christians are saved for two reasons: (1) to attain eternal life, and (2) to glorify God by their good deeds in society. The latter occurs as motivated responses of gratitude because of the promise in the eighth verse, "For by grace you have been saved through faith . . ." When Christians engage in good works, consistent with Ephesians 2:10, according to Wright, Christianity is more than just a religion.

Culture and Christians Accepting *Faith* and *Faiths*

The renowned cultural anthropologist Edward T. Hall has in-

99 Ibid.

100 Ibid.

sightfully noted, "Culture hides much more than it reveals, and what it hides, it hides most effectively from its own participants."[101] Thus, most humans—including Christians—are not usually conscious of how culture has influenced them to accept certain concepts and practices that sometimes contradict their beliefs and values. This phenomenon is also true regarding today's English-speaking Christians, who often use *faith* or *faiths* as synonyms for *religion* in conversations and publications, revealing that they have accepted their culture's concepts despite their being incompatible with the New Testament's use of *faith*.

As noted above, the word *faiths* first entered the English language in the 1800s and became more common in the 1900s. At this time, numerous Christians also began to speak of faiths instead of religions. One of the first noteworthy Christians to use the word *faiths* appears to have been Kenneth Latourette, a former Christian missionary in China and later a church history professor at Yale University. In 1937, he published the multivolume work *A History of Christianity: The First Five Centuries.* In this noteworthy work, he wrote about "one of the faiths" and "other faiths that had in them elements of truth."[102] But it was not until the latter half of the 1900s and the early twenty-first century that Christian authors regularly began referring to other religions as "faiths." Various Christian publishers soon followed suit by publishing books that used the word *faiths* in their books and book titles.

Consider these examples. In 1961, Stephen Neill, a former

101 Edward T. Hall, *The Silent Language* (Garden City, NY: Doubleday Books, 1959), 30.

102 Kenneth Scott Latourette, *A History of Christianity: The First Five Centuries* (New York: Harper Brothers, 1937), 1:65, 127.

Anglican missionary in India, published his book titled *Christian Faith and Other Faiths*. Another book, *Learning from Other Faiths* (2003), edited by several Christians, discusses some of the following: Abrahamic traditions, religion as a Western tradition, faith and politics in Islam, a Hindu response to the encyclical letter of *Fides et Ratio* (1998) by Pope John Paul II, and Western Buddhism. The book's title has *faiths* as a synonym for *religions*. These two books, published by Christian publishers, are only some of many that have failed to recognize that the word *faiths* is contrary to the New Testament, a reality that many Christian authors and publishing firms seem not to know or take seriously because of influence from their syncretistic culture.

The effect of this culture's influence is also seen in church-related publications and other media. To cite a noteworthy example, on October 5, 2018, the Rev. Robert James Jeffress Jr., a prominent clergyman of a large Baptist church in Dallas, Texas, was interviewed by Shannon Bream on Fox News. In defending Christianity, he said, "No *faith* has done more for women than Christianity, including Jesus" (emphasis added). Jeffress's comment clearly reveals his acceptance of the culture's biblically erroneous synonymizing of *faith* and *religion*. I cite him not as an exception but as an example among many Christians today who have unwittingly accepted the secular culture's faulty, unbiblical understanding of faith, unaware that this use of *faith* as a synonym for *religion* contradicts the New Testament's exclusive faith of Christianity.

Conclusion

In light of the numerous and incorrect faith phrases popular today, conscientious Christians need to refrain from voicing them. For example, Christians would do well to replace the phrase "people of faith" with "religiously minded people" and to replace "other faiths" with "other religions." They need to spurn the fallacious synonymizing of *faith* and *religion*, so common and widespread today. As G. K. Chesterton once wisely wrote, "Fallacies . . . do not cease to be fallacies because they become fashions."[103] Moreover, the synonymizing of *faith* and *religion* has no affinity to the exclusive faith of Christians.

For Christians to make this change in speaking and writing will not be easy. Culture is a powerful phenomenon that shapes people's behavior, especially their language, in unconscious ways. When new words or expressions are regularly heard in the culture, they soon become a part of everyday language and conversations. However, after learning of these contrabiblical faith phrases, will conscientious Christians seriously take on the biblically important task of correcting their speech? Or will they take the path of least resistance by continuing to go along with their culture, thus continuing to support the use of these contrabiblical concepts? If they opt for the latter, they unfortunately will not enhance the exclusive faith of Christianity.

---

103 G. K. Chesterton, *Illustrated London News*, April 19, 1930.

DISCUSSION QUESTIONS

1. What well-known liberal German theologian first synonymized *faith* and *religion*?
2. This same theologian also pluralized *faith* as *faiths*. What did this radical act do to the New Testament's use and meaning of faith?
3. When did these two radical innovations occur in the history of the Church?
4. Why was this same theologian not bothered theologically by his synonymizing of *faith* and *religion*?
5. What role did the Age of Enlightenment play in the synonymizing of *faith* and *religion* and the pluralizing of *faith*?
6. According to the New Testament, why is it theologically wrong for Christians to echo today's cultural practice of synonymizing *faith* and *religion*?
7. Why do so many Christians seem to accept the synonymizing of *faith* and *religion* and the pluralizing of *faith*?
8. What current political ideology in our Western culture advocates and promotes the synonymizing of *faith* and *religion*?
9. What role does our society's culture play in getting numerous well-meaning, devout Christians, contrary to the New Testament, to use *faiths* rather than *religions*?

10. Can you cite a Bible passage that urges Christians not to conform to cultural practices that are at odds with biblical values?

CHAPTER 4

FROM FAITH TO FIDEISM: A DECEPTIVE MISUSE OF FAITH

I suspect that most of the individuals who have religious faith are content with blind faith. They feel no obligation to understand what they believe.

Mortimer J. Adler, "A Philosopher's Religious Faith"

When Bible critics, prompted by the philosophy of the Enlightenment, hijacked faith from Christianity's exclusive use of faith based on the biblical, historical foundation of Christ's miracles and His bodily resurrection, they argued that faith was still valid for devout Christians if they sincerely believed that Christ's miracles and His resurrection had indeed occurred, even though both were only a reflection of what Christ's apostles in their eyes of faith reported in the four Gospels. Christianity's uniquely exclusive faith had now been radically redefined. Now faith had become faith based on no valid, historical evidence. It became merely faith in faith, better known as fideism.

Fideism Defined

Fideism has often been defined as faith that rejects all forms of reason, in contrast to the Bible critics who use reason to deny the historicity of Christ's miracles and His bodily resurrection as the valid, authentic foundation of the New Testament's exclusive faith. This is essentially how Alvin Plantinga sees fideism, when he refers to a dictionary's definition that says it is the "exclusive or basic reliance upon faith alone, accompanied by a consequent disparagement of reason and utilized especially in the pursuit of philosophical or religious truth."[104] He posits two kinds of fideism: moderate and extreme. The moderate type relies "upon faith rather than reason in religious matters," while the extreme type "disparages and denigrates reason."[105] But Teresa Morgan, Oxford University professor, has recently and correctly noted that fideism "deliberately eschews a basis in reason or evidence."[106] The rejection of evidence, as Morgan points out, is important for understanding the nature of fideism. It indicates that the Bible critics, who contend that faith is not based on the Bible's historical evidence, are thus the real fideists. In contrast, biblically guided Christians reject only unqualified or unrestrained reason, not all forms of it. Here it is important to remember that Christians, especially during the Protestant Reformation, saw faith as consisting of knowledge or evidence (*notitia*), assent (*assensus*), and trust (*fiducia*) in Christ's resurrection for life and eternal salvation.

These three elements of faith are consistent with reason, not opposed to it. The Early Church also employed reason and logic

104 Alvin Plantinga, "Reason and Belief in God," in Alvin Plantinga and Nicholas Wolterstorff, eds., *Faith and Rationality: Reason and Belief in God* (Notre Dame University Press, 1983), 87.

105 Ibid.

106 Teresa Morgan, *Roman Faith and Christian Faith* (Oxford: Oxford University Press, 2015), 149.

when it formulated certain doctrines. For example, at the Council of Nicaea in AD 325, Christian bishops rejected the heretical teachings of Arius, which denied the deity of Jesus Christ, when they formulated the Nicene Creed. This is only one example of how orthodox Christians used reason, rather than disparaged it, in defense of Christianity's biblical teachings.

Hijacking faith from its biblically reliable, historical knowledge, as the Bible critics have done and continue to do, is quite consistent with fideism. This has not been recognized or admitted by the critics, who have accepted the lamentable hijacking of faith from its biblical, historical evidence, and thus they often wrongly accuse conservative Christians of rejecting reason and see them as guilty of fideism. But ironically, what the biblical critics and liberal theologians today call faith, which is not based on evidence, is fideism. That is the only logical way one can understand what Bible critics like Richard Simon, Gotthold Lessing, David Friedrich Strauss, Martin Kähler, Paul Tillich, Rudolf Bultmann, Karl Barth, and Dietrich Bonhoeffer taught and advocated regarding faith, as cited in chapter 2. They saw faith as a phenomenon not linked to empirical, historical evidence. Hence, their concept of faith is best described as faith in faith, or fideism.

Varied Hues of Fideism

Books, articles, and conversations all offer a glimpse into the various ways Christianity's exclusive faith is misunderstood or wrongly perceived. The following examples show the various hues of fideism advocated by various individuals today.

"Faith Is Not Based on Facts"

We now live in a culture where people (including many misinformed, undiscerning Christians) speak about faith as a phenomenon that "has little or no connection with an intelligent appraisal of facts," as Norman Anderson has shown. He rightly called this perception "a grave misconception."[107] It is not difficult to find this erroneous, antibiblical view of faith expressed in many venues today. Hence, an editorial published in the periodical *Biblical Archaeology Review* (July/August 2010) stated, "Facts are facts, and faith has no business dealing with the world of facts. Faith resides in the heart and in one's way of living in the world."[108] Clearly, if one's faith is not based on facts, then logically one can have only faith in faith, and that is fideism. This editorial is an example of how faith is erroneously perceived by many today.

Faith not based on facts, as often expressed in liberal theology and in the secular media, conflicts with the requirement Jesus' eleven apostles used to select a person to replace the traitor Judas Iscariot. The Book of Acts states the prospective apostle to replace Judas had to be someone who had seen Christ after He had risen from the dead (Acts 1:21–23). Mere faith without the prospective candidate having seen the resurrected Christ was not an acceptable option. Thus, two men, Justus and Matthias, who both had seen the bodily resurrected Jesus Christ were proposed. The eleven apostles

107 Norman Anderson, *Jesus Christ: The Witness of History* (Downers Grove, IL: InterVarsity Press, 1985), 151.

108 Ronald Hendel, "Farewell to SBL: Faith and Reason in Biblical Studies," *Biblical Archaeology Review* (July/August, 2010), 28.

then cast lots that resulted in the selection of Matthias (Acts 1:26) to bring their number back to twelve apostles.

If the faith of Christians is independent of the factual knowledge of Christ's miracles and His bodily resurrection, as the Bible critics argue, devout Christians then ask, why did Jesus after His resurrection reveal Himself physically (about a dozen times) to His disciples? On one occasion, He even ate some broiled fish in their presence (Luke 24:42–43). Hence, it can be argued that Christ's appearing physically to His disciples after His resurrection was in part done to strengthen their faith in Him. Here it is important to recall the words of John the apostle: "Now Jesus did many other signs in the presence of the disciples, which are not written in this book; but these are written so that you may believe that Jesus is the Christ, the Son of God, and that by believing you may have life in His name" (John 20:30–31).

The presuppositional argument of the Bible critics who contend that faith is independent of the historical knowledge or evidence recorded in the Bible is rejected by conservative biblical scholars. These Christian scholars agree with the German scholar Wolfhart Pannenberg, who has cogently stated, "The proclamation of the Gospel cannot assert that the facts are in doubt and that a leap of faith must be made to achieve certainty. If this sort of assertion were allowed, then one would have to cease being a theologian and a Christian." Thus, he concluded, "The proclamation must assert that the facts are reliable and that you can therefore place your faith, life, and future on them."[109] Further countering the fideism of

109 Wolfhart Pannenberg, *Revelation as History*, trans. David Granskow (Philadelphia: The Macmillan Company, 1968), 138.

the Bible critics, Pannenberg asserted, "A person does not come to faith blindly, but by means of an event that can be appropriated as something that can be considered reliable. True faith is not a state of blissful gullibility."[110]

"To Believe Is Not the Same as to Know"

When the radical 1960s were unfolding, the president of a theological seminary in St. Paul, Minnesota, wrote an article "Now, about Faith" in a periodical for Lutheran youth. The author, Alvin Rogness, boldly stated, "To know is not the same as to believe; to believe is not the same as to know. In fact, if you know something, you no longer need to believe it." He continued, "There really are two worlds: the world of knowing and the world of believing. In the world of knowing, the evidences or the proofs are beyond question. In the world of believing, the evidences are not yet in. In fact, there may never be proofs that will be generally accepted."[111]

This article contradicts the New Testament's assurance that a Christian's faith is based on the knowledge that Jesus Christ conquered sin and death by His crucifixion and by rising from the dead three days later. The article makes no mention of the important role this knowledge played in prompting Thomas, for instance, to change from an entrenched skeptic to a firm professor of faith upon seeing the crucifixion wounds of the risen Christ. This encounter moved him to say, "My Lord and my God!" (John 20:28), prompted by the empirical experience of seeing the risen Lord who told Thomas to see and touch His body's crucifixion wounds. Thus,

110 Ibid.

111 Alvin Rogness, "Now, about Faith," *Arena One* (January 1967), 4.

the idea that "if you know something, you no longer need to believe it" is false. If this statement were true, then logically speaking, the apostle Thomas did not utter words of faith when he declared, "My Lord and my God!" upon seeing the risen Christ, for Thomas now had factual, visible knowledge that Christ had truly risen from the dead.

This article is also wrong given what the apostles Peter and John told the religious authorities in Jerusalem who had ordered them to cease proclaiming Christ's bodily resurrection. They responded, "We cannot but speak of what we have seen and heard" (Acts 4:20). Their response was a proclamation of their faith based on their eyewitness knowledge of having seen and heard their risen Lord. The article's assertion that faith is not based on knowledge also contradicts the Protestant Reformation's teaching that defined biblical faith as consisting of *notitia* (knowledge), *assensus* (assent), and *fiducia* (trust).

Also important to note is the fact that the historical knowledge of Christ's bodily resurrection and its related events were unequivocally accepted as authentic by the early Christians. They commemorated and marked the dates of these events on their calendar. Eusebius, the fourth-century Church historian, states that in about AD 154, Bishop Polycarp from Asia Minor met with Bishop Anicetus in Rome regarding the dispute that existed among churches with respect to when *Pascha* (the Greek name for Christ's death and resurrection) was to be celebrated. Churches in the West celebrated Christ's resurrection on Sunday; churches in the East celebrated it on the fourteenth day of Nisan (Jewish month of April), which meant that Easter Day (*Pascha*) could fall on any day of the week. The Council of Nicaea (AD 325) finally settled the dispute in favor of the Western Church's position.

The disagreement among early Christians as to when Easter was to be celebrated indicates the historical significance Christ's bodily resurrection had for them. It was the physical appearance of Christ after His resurrection that verified the reality of His resurrection to the apostles and to more than five hundred individuals who saw Him after He had risen from the dead (see 1 Corinthians 15:5–8). There was also the empty tomb, a phenomenon that all four Gospels underscore. All those who wanted to see the empty tomb could see it, if they so desired. In short, the four Gospel writers did not write about the resurrection from hearsay information. As Karl Adam has rightly noted, "[The apostles] had learned of His resurrection by way of sober sense-perception, which is the only guarantee of genuine objective, empirical knowledge."[112]

Given the empirical knowledge that Christ's apostles and some of their contemporaries possessed and valued, it is amazing that there are today some prominent Christians (influenced by the skepticism of historical-critical scholars) who not only divorce faith from knowledge for themselves, but also try to persuade others (as does Rogness's article cited above) that Christians must keep faith separate and distinct from knowledge.

Many devout Christians, unwittingly and erringly, express themselves regarding Christ's resurrection by echoing the non-

112 Karl Adam, *The Christ of Faith: The Christology of the Church*, trans. Joyce Crick (New York: Pantheon Books, 1957), 350.

knowledge basis of faith. As an example, permit me to note a comment once uttered by Peter L. Berger, a liberal Lutheran and renowned American sociologist of religion. Speaking of Christ's bodily resurrection, he stated, "But to say that Christ is risen requires faith. It is not something I know."[113] Berger's statement indicates that he accepts the Bible critics' argument that Christ's resurrection is not based on reliable, factual knowledge. Thus, he must have faith to accept Christ's bodily resurrection. His response is a response of fideism, a widely unrecognized misuse of faith today.

Contrary to Berger, to accept Christ's resurrection from the dead does not require faith. It is only the acceptance of the spiritual benefits of Christ's resurrection that require faith, not whether the resurrection happened as an event in history. The latter has been historically corroborated by the eyewitness accounts of Christ's apostles who suffered death and imprisonment but never wavered in their testimony. Thus, the historical authenticity of Christ's resurrection is firmly linked to knowledge, not to faith.

Many committed Christians who do not accept the argument that faith is separate from knowledge, however, often unwittingly indicate that their faith is not linked to knowledge when they say, "I *believe* that Christ rose from the dead." When a devout Christian makes this statement, an alert Christian friend would be right in asking, "Do you mean that you do not *know* that Christ rose from the dead?" By asking this question, the questioner rightly indicates that, biblically speaking, the faith of Christians is based on *know-*

113 Peter L. Berger, "An Interview with Peter Berger: Choosing Our Religion," *Modern Reformation* (January–February 2010), 32.

ing that Christ died and rose from the dead, rather than merely *believing* that He rose from the dead. Yet the statement "I *believe* that Christ rose from the dead" is usually accepted by pastors and churches as though it were a biblically correct response, when in fact it is biblically incorrect. For it is not a Christian's faith that makes Christ's resurrection true. Rather, it is the historical, factual knowledge of His resurrection that makes the Christian's faith true and valid.

Consider this analogous example. Suppose an American citizen were to say, "I *believe* that George Washington was the first president of the United States." Any hearer would be correct in asking, "Do you not *know* that George Washington was the first president of the United States?" Whether Jesus rose from the dead or whether Washington was the first president of the United States is not a matter of anyone's belief or faith, but whether the event or the person's office has been corroborated by reliable, historical knowledge. Thus, it is incorrect to say, "I *believe* that Washington was the first president," and similarly it is incorrect to say, "I *believe* that Christ rose from the dead." This is not how the apostles who had seen the risen Christ spoke of His resurrection.

To be sure, it is biblically correct for the Christian to confess, "I believe in the resurrection of the body," as stated in the Apostles' Creed. For here the Christian is referring to his or her future bodily resurrection, and thus it is an expression of faith. But when a Christian says, "I believe that Christ rose from the dead," it is biblically incorrect, as just noted. For this statement falsely indicates that Christ's resurrection is only a matter of faith, ignoring that the faith of Christians in the New Testament includes their *knowing* the eyewitness reports of Christ's apostles that reveal Christ's bodily resurrection as an event that occurred in history. The important fact that the faith of Christians in the New Testament includes *knowing* that Christ rose from the dead has unfortunately not been recognized for the longest time by all too many Christians and their church leaders. This unrecognized aspect of faith—namely, that Christians *knew* Christ rose from the dead as part of their faith—helps explain why every year on Easter Sunday we hear the mass media report, "Christians believe that Christ rose from the dead on this day." This statement implies Christians see Christ's resurrection as a mere faith event, devoid of reliable historical knowledge. There is no mention of Christ's apostles having reported what they *knew* from having personally interacted with their risen Lord. Given this faulty reporting of Easter, compatible with the Bible critics' hijacked view of faith, it is salutary to know that Samuel Medley appropriately titled his biblically based hymn "I Know That My Redeemer Lives."

Regarding the role of faith linked to knowledge, faith accepts the *effects* or the *benefits* of Christ's bodily resurrection. However, it was not the faith of the apostles that established the veracity of Christ's resurrection. Rather, it was His resurrection that established and grounded their faith. That is why Peter declared, "This Jesus God raised up, and of that we all are witnesses" (Acts 2:32). Later, Peter and John made it resoundingly clear when they defied the religious authorities who demanded they cease talking about Christ's bodily resurrection, to which they responded, "We cannot but speak what we have seen and heard" (Acts 4:20). They spoke of what they *knew* was factually true, rather than what they *believed* to be true.

Given the copious biblical evidence that the faith of the apostles included their *knowing* that Christ had risen from the dead, and their having publicly vouched for this empirical knowledge, it is disappointing to see how a liberal theologian (cited above) could tell readers that "to believe is not the same as to know." Clearly, he echoed the rationalistic presupposition of the Bible critics who contend that faith cannot be linked to what is recorded in the Bible as factual knowledge.

This presupposition that teaches faith is independent of knowledge is widespread today among many scholars and liberally minded Christians, and it makes little or no difference to what denomination they belong. Thus, the American Roman Catholic novelist Flannery O'Connor, in her response to a college student who had heard one of her lectures in which she mentioned the concept of faith, replied to her, "Faith is what you have in the absence of knowledge."[114] Her perception of faith is another unfortunate example of fideism, namely, faith hijacked from its reliable, biblical knowledge.

The separation of faith from knowledge has sometimes been shockingly expressed. For instance, philosopher Immanuel Kant rejected knowledge as the basis of faith: "I have therefore found it necessary to deny *knowledge* [sic], in order to make room for *faith*

---

114 Flannery O'Connor, *The Habit of Being: Letters*, ed. Sally Fitzgerald (New York: Vintage Books, 1980), 387.

[sic]."[115] Kant's opting for faith as independent of its knowledge base is another example of fideism.

"Faith Is Illogical Belief"

American journalist Henry L. Mencken once wrote, "Faith may be defined briefly as an illogical belief in the occurrence of the improbable."[116] Mencken's definition assumes that faith is "illogical" because it is based on what he calls "the occurrence of the improbable." To him, faith is believing in faith. But his definition is false because it ignores that Christianity's concept of faith rests on the empirical phenomenon of Christ's bodily resurrection that did indeed occur in history. To repeat what I have stated before, it was an event that was publicly verified by Christ's eyewitnesses, His apostles, and seen by more than five hundred persons (1 Corinthians 15:6).

"Leap of Faith"

This phrase, now widely used by liberal theologians, originated with Soren Kierkegaard, a Danish religious philosopher of Lutheran background. It commonly indicates that an individual believes something for which there is no evidence or reliable knowledge, thus blind faith. Although Kierkegaard's use of this term is a bit more nuanced in that he argued the "ugly ditch" that Gotthold Lessing posed could be crossed by taking what he called "the leap of faith," it nevertheless fits the meaning of fideism rather well.[117]

---

115 Immanuel Kant, *Critique of Pure Reason*, trans. Norman Kemp Smith (New York: St. Martin's Press, 1929), 29.

116 Henry L. Mencken, *Prejudices: Third Series* (New York: Knopf, 1924), 267.

117 Lessing expressed his "ugly ditch" as follows: "Accidental truths of history can never become proofs for the necessary truths of reason."

The so-called leap of faith is a veiled way of saying faith is not based on fact, and thus it requires a blind leap. This concept has no biblical basis or precedents. It even contradicts biblical examples of individuals who publicly revealed their faith. When the Roman centurion, standing before Christ on the cross, said, "Truly this man was the Son of God!" (Mark 15:39), he did not take a leap of faith. Rather, it was what he had heard and seen, right in front of him, that prompted him to declare his faith. Similarly, Thomas's response of "My Lord and my God!" (John 20:28) upon seeing the risen Christ was also not a leap of faith. Rather, it was the visible, empirical evidence that God's Holy Spirit used to move him to utter these words of faith. For as the apostle Paul said, "No one can say 'Jesus is Lord' except in the Holy Spirit" (1 Corinthians 12:3). In short, the New Testament knows nothing about any Christians having taken a "leap of faith."

"Faith Requires No Evidence"

A related argument is the idea that faith requires no evidence, as Sam Harris in his book *The End of Faith* makes bold to say: "Every religion preaches the truth of propositions for which it has no evidence."[118] This assertion indicates Harris either does not know or rejects the Christian exception, namely, the historical, empirical evidence of Jesus Christ's bodily resurrection. For Christianity has from its beginning consistently taught that Christ did indeed rise from the dead, but if He did not, the faith of Christians would be null and void. That is why the apostle Paul told those in the Co-

118 Sam Harris, *The End of Faith: Religion, Terror, and the Future of Reason* (New York: W. W. Norton and Company, 2004), 23.

rinthian Church who doubted Christ's resurrection, "If Christ has not been raised, then our preaching is in vain and your faith in vain" (1 Corinthians 15:14). To further gainsay the skeptics, Paul pointed to courtroom-like evidence by asserting that more than five hundred individuals, most of whom were still alive; the apostles; James, the brother of Jesus; and Paul himself had seen the risen Lord (1 Corinthians 15:6–8). This certainly is evidence, and it is uniquely Christian.

Still, some may ask, "What about Hebrews 11:1?" This reference reads, "Now faith is the assurance of things hoped for, the conviction of things not seen." Some use this passage to argue that the faith of Christians is not based on any evidence. But that is not what this passage says. For the early Hebrew Christians, soon after Christ had risen from the dead, knew His bodily resurrection was a historical fact. It was not something they accepted on blind faith without evidence. Thus, this passage speaks only about the effects or the benefits of Christ's resurrection, namely, obtaining the promise of eternal life. That is what these Hebrew Christians were hoping for but could not yet see or experience. In short, this reference does not support blind faith without evidence, as some mistakenly contend.

Moreover, if faith is only "the conviction of things not seen," as stated in the Hebrews passage, then Christ's apostles, including Thomas after his confession, had a dubious faith. For Peter, speaking on behalf of the apostles, expressed his and their faith, by saying, "This Jesus God raised up, and of that we all are witnesses"

(Acts 2:32). Their faith was not based "on the conviction of things not seen."

If the faith of Christians has no empirical, evidential foundation, they are then, as one observant Christian has rightly stated, "in company with the queen in *Alice in Wonderland* who could believe half a dozen impossible things before breakfast."[119] This analogy of the queen in Lewis Carroll's novel is a revealing portrait of many well-meaning but misinformed Christians who today have unwittingly accepted liberal theology's nonevidential view of faith. Thus, it is important to note that accepting the validity of faith without evidence logically means it can also be dismissed or discredited without evidence, for faith in nothing is still nothing.

To argue that faith requires no evidence ignores that Jesus valued the importance of empirical evidence to bolster the faith of His followers. He once told skeptics to consider "the evidence of [His] works [that is, His miracles]" (John 14:11 NIV) that He had performed because they did not believe what He had said about His divine identity. Similarly, when John the Baptist was locked in prison, he sent his disciples to ask Jesus, "Are You the one who is to come, or shall we look for another?" (Matthew 11:3). Jesus told them, "Go and tell John what you hear and see: the blind receive their sight and the lame walk, lepers are cleansed and the deaf hear, and the dead are raised up, and the poor have good news preached to them" (Matthew 11:4–5). In short, Jesus did not tell them that John just needed to have faith that He was the Promised One. Instead, He pointed to empirical evidence of His miraculous

119 Stephen Board, "Fact and Faith in Modern Theology," *Christianity Today* (May 26, 1967), 8.

works to buttress John's weak faith. Hence, for some to say that faith needs no evidence clashes with Jesus' own words and actions.

In a similar vein, Luke underscored the importance of evidence for the faith of the early Christians. Luke told them that after Christ had risen from the dead He appeared to His apostles, giving them "many infallible proofs, being seen by them during forty days" (Acts 1:3 NKJV). That Christ appeared to and interacted with His apostles multiple times during the forty days before His ascension also indicates that He wanted them to have the empirical evidence of His bodily resurrection to buttress their faith. He knew their faith would be severely tested and they would even experience persecution for their preaching and teaching the historical reality and the purpose of His bodily resurrection after He had commanded them to take this message to different parts of the world (Matthew 28:19–20).

However, the significance Christ placed on the importance of evidence for the validity of faith has not been taught well in many churches. Thus, many Christians mistakenly think faith is essentially blind and needs no evidence, an erroneous conclusion that has been a part of our Western culture since the so-called Enlightenment. This conclusion is contrary not only to what Christ taught but also to what is underscored by the apostles Paul, Peter, and John.

As noted above, in 1 Corinthians 15, Paul argued for the veracity of Christ's bodily resurrection by citing empirical evidence. Peter urged the early Christians to always be "prepared to make a defense to anyone who asks you for a reason for the hope that is in you" (1 Peter 3:15). By making "a defense," he meant they needed to point to reliable evidence. The apostle John assured the recipients of his first epistle that he and his fellow apostles had "seen with our eyes, which we looked upon and have touched with our hands, concerning the word of life" (1 John 1:1). John also understood the value of evidence from another experience he had: when he came to Christ's empty tomb, he "went in, and he saw and believed" (John 20:8). His previous personal interactions with his Lord, together with his seeing the empty tomb, gave him a firm basis for his faith, far removed from the blind faith of fideism.

"Evidential Faith is Inferior Faith"

Noteworthy is the degree to which Christianity's exclusive faith in the New Testament has been hijacked from the historical evidence of Christ's miracles and His bodily resurrection, as espoused by Bible critics of the higher-critical methodology since the Age of the Enlightenment. This faulty view of faith is now accepted by many misguided Christians, as J. Warner Wallace has recently made known:

> I often encounter devoted, committed Christians who are hesitant to embrace an *evidential* faith. In many Christian circles, faith that requires evidential support is seen as weak and inferior. For many, *blind faith* (a faith that simply trusts without question) is the truest, most sincere, and most valuable form of faith.[120]

This contrabiblical view of faith unfortunately comports well

120 J. Warner Wallace, *Cold-Case Christianity* (Colorado Springs: David C. Cook, 2013), 53.

with what many contemporary clergy and theologians now accept as faith for themselves and for today's church members. Given the determination to separate faith from historical evidence, some argue, "What must go is the assumption that faith must be grounded in factual historical events."[121] They want faith in faith, thus fideism, although they do not call it that.

Others with similar convictions contend that Christian apologists place too much emphasis on the doctrine that Christianity's exclusive faith is solely based on the Bible's historical event of Christ's bodily resurrection. They argue if it were ever proven that Christ did not rise from the dead, it could destroy Christianity. Hence, blind faith (fideism) in their minds is not an enemy of the faith of Christians but its potential guardian.

To these liberally minded Christians who do not want Christian apologists to defend the biblical, historical foundation of Christ's bodily resurrection, it must be emphatically stated that if such contrary evidence were ever discovered, it would indeed destroy Christianity, and well it should. For faith not linked to the historicity of Christ's miracles and His bodily resurrection is not the faith found and taught in the New Testament. Nor is such "faith" a part of biblical Christianity. That kind of faith would be a fake faith, and thus a fake Christianity.

For some to think that Christianity would still be Christian if such evidence proved that Christ did not rise from the dead totally departs from the heart and core of biblical Christianity. For authentic Christianity stands or falls with the empirical, historical

121 C. Stephen Evans, *Kierkegaard on Faith and the Self* (Waco, TX: Baylor University Press, 2006), 154.

reality that Christ did indeed rise from the dead. As Paul declared, "If Christ has not been raised, your faith is futile and you are still in your sins. Then those also who have fallen asleep in Christ have perished. If in Christ we have hope in this life only, we are of all people most to be pitied" (1 Corinthians 15:17–19).

Liberal Christians who fear that future evidence might reveal Christ did not rise from the dead evidently do not accept the eyewitness accounts of Christ's apostles in the New Testament as historically true. They want a Christianity immune to any possible evidence that would prove Christ did not rise from the grave. But if the exclusive faith of Christians, which is based on the veracity of Christ's bodily resurrection, were immune to any possible evidence disproving His resurrection, Christianity would be merely a make-believe religion. It would leave its followers eternally destitute, like the followers of all non-Christian religions. But faith based on Christ's bodily resurrection makes Christianity unique and authentic. It gives substance and meaning to Jesus' words, well-known to numerous Christians, "For God so loved the world, that He gave His only Son, that whoever believes in Him should not perish but have eternal life" (John 3:16), and provides assurance from the words Peter spoke, "There is salvation in no one else, for there is no other name under heaven given among men by which we must be saved" (Acts 4:12).

"Jesus Lives in My Heart"

Sometimes when the faith of some well-meaning Christians is challenged, it is not uncommon to hear them say, "I know that my faith is true and certain because Jesus lives in my heart." This is not only an emotional expression but also a remark of fideism, for it is not the feelings a Christian has in his or her heart that make faith true and certain, but whether his or her faith is based on the deeds of Christ, especially His crucifixion and bodily resurrection that occurred as empirical events in history.

The certainty of Christ's deeds, crucifixion, and resurrection does not depend on any Christian's faith. Rather, it is Christ's deeds and resurrection that make the Christian's faith true and authentic. The certainty of faith comes not from faith but from outside of faith. As Wolfhart Pannenberg has correctly noted, "Faith cannot ascertain anything certain about events of the past that would be inaccessible to the historian."[122] That is why Paul told skeptics in Corinth that the risen Christ had "appeared to more than five hundred brothers at one time, most of whom are still alive" (1 Corinthians 15:6). In short, he told the skeptics it was not faith that made Christ's resurrection certain. If they wanted certainty, his statement indicates they could ask some of the individuals of the more than five hundred who had visually seen the risen Jesus Christ.

"The Burning in Your Bosom"

When Mormons are challenged about the authenticity of their professed teachings, they have been taught to cite Joseph Smith's purported revelation from God. It states,

> But, behold, I say unto you, that you must study it out in your mind; then you must ask me if it be right, and

122 Wolfhart Pannenberg, *Jesus—God and Man*, trans. Lewis Wilkins and Duane A. Priebe (Philadelphia: The Westminster Press, 1968), 109.

> if it is right, I will cause that *your bosom* shall burn within you; therefore, you shall feel that it is right. But if it be not right you shall have no such feelings, but you shall have a stupor of thought that shall cause you to forget the thing which is wrong; therefore, you cannot write that which is sacred save it be given you from me. (*Doctrine and Covenants* 9:8–9, emphasis added)

There is no appeal in Joseph Smith's revelation to any external, verified evidence underlying a Mormon's presumed faith. The response is merely a subjective utterance of blind faith and thus another hue in the spectrum of fideism.

"Faith Is Independent of the Five Senses"

Modern examples of fideism are not voiced only by liberally minded individuals. For example, a conservative pastor once explained Christian faith this way: "Faith means believing something is true without the benefit of the five senses. If the senses (feeling, tasting, seeing, smelling, or hearing) are involved, the belief is no longer based on faith, but on a fact."[123] This is clearly an antibiblical definition of faith. If this definition were biblically correct, Thomas's confession of "My Lord and my God!" (John 20:28) would have been a faithless remark, because his confession was prompted by what he *saw* and *felt* with two of his five senses, seeing and touching Christ's resurrected body.

This example of fideism reveals that even a conservative pastor immersed in today's liberal culture can adopt an antibiblical view

123 Jack Cascione, "Wise Men Act on Faith," *Christian News* (January 5, 1998), 24.

of faith, one that is now widely accepted in the liberal theology of numerous Protestant and Roman Catholic churches.

"Faith without Content or Object"

In 1955, President Dwight D. Eisenhower told Americans that their religious faith was the most basic expression of Americanism: "Our government makes no sense unless it is founded in a deeply felt religious faith—and I don't care what it is."[124] In response to this statement, David Yount has rightly noted, "The president was indifferent as to the content and object of faith as long as all citizens believed."[125] Yount further stated that this view of faith coincided with Americans merely having "faith in faith—the positive and comforting attitude of *believing*—and not much more."[126] This is an unmistakable example of fideism.

Sola Fide (Faith Alone)

Although chapter 1 briefly discussed the concept of *sola fide* as an integral part of Christianity's exclusive faith, it is fitting also to mention it in this chapter, primarily so readers do not mistakenly conclude that *sola fide* is just another hue of fideism. To the contrary, the *sola fide* concept is firmly linked to Christ's atoning words and deeds that occurred as empirical events in history.

Early in the days of the Reformation, Martin Luther invoked the concept of *sola fide* to underscore the biblical teaching that Christians were saved not by both faith and good works but

124 Cited in Will Herberg, *Protestant—Catholic—Jew: An Essay in American Religious Sociology* (Garden City: Doubleday and Company, 1955), 84.

125 David Yount, *The Future of Christian Faith in America* (Minneapolis: Augsburg Fortress, 2004), 2.

126 Ibid.

through faith in Christ alone, based on His death and bodily resurrection that had occurred in history. Luther leaned on the inspired words of the apostle Paul, who told the Corinthian Christians, "If Christ has not been raised, then our preaching is in vain and your faith is in vain" (1 Corinthians 15:14). The factual event of Christ's resurrection moved the apostle Paul to tell the Christians in Rome, "For we hold that one is justified by faith apart from works of the law" (Romans 3:28). In short, nowhere in the copious literature of the Reformation pertaining to *sola fide* does it denote any aspects of faith independent of biblically based historical evidence that would be akin to blind faith or fideism.

Conclusion

As noted in chapter 2, the liberal argument that faith is independent of biblical, historical knowledge is the product of the Enlightenment's Bible critics, who argued that the faith of Christians would not be harmed if Christ's miracles and bodily resurrection did not happen in history. They contended that those accounts were the product of His apostles, who in their faith and admiration of Jesus reported what they personally believed and admired rather than what had empirically taken place. In short, according to the Bible critics, the reports of Christ's apostles are not historically anchored or factually true.

Regarding the blind faith of fideism, American philosopher of religion Mortimer J. Adler has stated that most religious individuals "feel no obligation to understand what they believe. They may wish not to have their beliefs disturbed by thought. But if God in whom they believe created them with intellectual and rational powers, that imposes on them the duty to try to understand the creed of their religion. Not to do so is to verge on superstition."[127]

Closely related to Adler's assessment is the comment voiced by Chad Walsh. He contends that "millions of Christians live in a sentimental haze of vague piety, with soft organ music trembling in the lovely light from stained-glass windows. Their religion is a thing of pleasant emotional quivers, divorced from the will, divorced from the intellect, and demanding little except lip service to a few harmless platitudes."[128]

Earlier in this chapter, we saw that the apostle Peter urged the early Christians "to make a defense to anyone who asks you for a reason for the hope that is in you" (1 Peter 3:15). Thus, to whatever extent the comments by Adler and Walsh are true, they reflect an unfortunate departure from the faith Peter had, anchored in the historical event of Christ's bodily resurrection. It was not the so-called "faith" of fideism that prompted Peter to pen those commanding and encouraging words.

127 Mortimer J. Adler, "A Religious Philosopher's Faith," in Kelly James Clark, ed., *Philosophers Who Believe: The Spiritual Journeys of Eleven Leading Thinkers* (Downers Grove, IL: InterVarsity Press, 1993), 207.

128 Chad Walsh, *Early Christians of the Twenty-First Century* (New York: Harper and Brothers, 1950), 11.

DISCUSSION QUESTIONS

1. What is having faith in faith formally and theologically called?
2. Why is the Lutheran Reformation principle of *sola fide* (by faith alone) not an example of fideism?
3. Why is the statement "to believe is not the same as to know" an example of fideism?
4. Why is the expression "leap of faith," often heard from some Christians today, an example of fideism?
5. How does the well-known hymn "I Know That My Redeemer Lives" counter fideism?
6. When the disciples of the doubting John the Baptist came to Jesus, Jesus did not say, "Go tell him to have more faith." Instead, Jesus pointed him to the many miraculous works He had performed. Why are Jesus' words the opposite of fideism?
7. What would a fideist-minded Christian most likely have told John the Baptist's disciples?
8. Chapter 4 includes various examples of fideism. Can you cite two?
9. Some liberal Christians fear that future evidence might prove Christ did not rise from the dead and therefore contend that we should not defend His resurrection's historical authenticity. Why is this an argument of fideism?

CHAPTER 5

IDIOSYNCRATIC VIEWS OF FAITH: THE SUBJECTIVE MISUSE OF FAITH

People almost invariably arrive at their beliefs not on the basis of proof but on the basis of what they find attractive.

Blaise Pascal, "On the Art of Persuasion"

As noted earlier, the concept of faith is widely used today in books and articles, but it is rarely defined. One would, however, expect to find it defined in sermons preached in Christian churches and in church publications. Such is not the case. In 1925, Presbyterian theologian and professor J. Gresham Machen criticized clergy for not defining *faith*: "These preachers speak about faith, but they do not tell what faith is."[129] He also stated, "If that question [what is faith?] were rightly answered, the Church . . . would soon emerge from its perplexities and would go forth with a new joy to the conquest of the world."[130]

Little or nothing has changed since Machen voiced his criticism. One only needs to ask, when have you, as a church-attending Christian, heard your pastor in sermons, or in other church con-

129 J. Gresham Machen, *What Is Faith?* (Grand Rapids: Eerdmans, 1925), 43.

130 Ibid., 40.

texts, define faith for you and other church members? Yet the word *faith* is used in sermons, in prayers, and in hymns in every Christian church every week, but it is safe to say that scores of Christians have never heard the concept of faith formally defined. Thus, they do not know, as Machen says, what faith is.

The void of faith definitions prompts two questions: (1) Do Christian clergy assume their parishioners know what faith is and thus see no need to define it? (2) Are the clergy content with whatever their parishioners might think faith is, regardless of how inadequate or erroneous their understanding of faith might be? If the answer to these questions is yes, it may help explain why so many idiosyncratic views of faith are expressed in the public media and by well-known individuals.

Examples of Idiosyncratic Views of Faith

Today's numerous and varied views (not real definitions) of faith in countless books and articles can often best be described as examples of their authors' idiosyncrasies, which reflect their personal, subjective feelings and worldview. What they call faith is the product of their not knowing or understanding the nature and role that faith played in the lives of early Christians in the New Testament, where it functioned as an exclusive religious phenomenon that had Jesus Christ as its source and object. This faith was linked to Christ's crucifixion and bodily resurrection. It distinguished His followers from "the ones of no faith" (*oi apistoi*), whom Paul mentions "the god of this world has blinded" so that they do not see "the light of the gospel of the glory of Christ, who is the image of God" (2 Corinthians 4:4).

"Faith Is Believing What Ain't So"

Although worded slightly differently, a schoolboy character in one of Mark Twain's writings once said, "Faith is believing what you know ain't so."[131] This is perhaps one of the more widely known idiosyncratic expressions of faith. In Mark Twain's day, most Americans would most likely not have said this about faith, but given Twain's skepticism and idiosyncratic disposition, this remark said more about him than about his biblically uninformed, facetious view of faith.

"Faith Is Ultimate Concern"

The liberal German theologian Paul Tillich once said, "There is hardly a word in the religious language, both theological and popular, which is subject to more misunderstandings, distortions, and questionable definitions than the word 'faith.'"[132] In this regard, Tillich was right. However, he still added his own incomprehensible definition: "Faith is a total and centered act of the personal self, the act of unconditional, infinite and ultimate concern. . . . The unconditional concern which is faith is the concern about the unconditional. The infinite passion, as faith has been described, is the passion for the infinite."[133]

Tillich's definition of faith is essentially incomprehensible. It merely reveals an idiosyncratic view of faith with no biblical basis.

131 Albert Bigelow Paine, *Mark Twain's Notebook* (New York: Harper's, 1935), 237.

132 Paul Tillich, *Dynamics of Faith* (New York: Harper and Brothers, 1957), ix

133 Ibid., 8–9.

"FAITH IS NONRATIONAL"

Still another idiosyncratic view of faith has been voiced by Jon Krakauer, author of the book *Under the Banner of Heaven* about Mormonism. Krakauer wrote: "All religious belief is a function of nonrational faith. And faith, by its very definition, tends to be impervious to intellectual argument or academic criticism."[134] Here Krakauer, like the Bible critics, argues that the faith of all religious adherents is not based on verifiable evidence. While Krakauer's argument is true for Mormonism and all other non-Christian religions, it is wrong and not valid with respect to Christianity's concept of faith. Christianity is the only religion whose faith is based on reliable, historical knowledge, contrary to what Bible critics argue when they ignore scholarly evidence, such as F. F. Bruce's book *Are the New Testament Documents Reliable?*[135] In this well-documented book, Bruce showed that the New Testament's books are indeed historically reliable, similar to other historically corroborated books. Then in 1978, Bruce reinforced his earlier evidence for the reliability of the Bible's New Testament Scriptures in the article "Are the New Testament Documents Still Reliable?" As might be surmised, the answer to this question again was a resounding yes.[136]

Krakauer's argument that "faith, by its very definition, tends to be impervious to intellectual argument or academic criticism" also fails to tell us what that "very definition" is. His not giving a

134 Jon Krakauer, *Under the Banner of Heaven* (New York: Doubleday 2003), 68.

135 F. F. Bruce, *Are the New Testament Documents Reliable?* (Grand Rapids: Wm. B. Eerdmans Publishing Company, 1954).

136 F. F. Bruce, "Are the New Testament Documents Still Reliable?" *Christianity Today* (October 28, 1978), 28–33.

definition is another example of what many authors do today when they write or speak of faith: they fail to define it. They apparently assume that everyone intuitively knows what the nature of faith is. But as the various idiosyncrasies in this chapter reveal, that assumption is notably incorrect.

"Biblical 'Facts' as Faith"

In response to the opening of the Bible Museum in Washington, DC, *The Economist* published an editorial critical of the purpose of the Bible Museum. Reflecting an idiosyncratic view of faith, the author wrote, "Arguably, even talking about the 'facts' of the Bible is a statement of faith, and one with unusual resonance in America."[137] For the author to say that "facts" in the Bible are items of faith assumes everything written in the Bible has no factual basis, a conclusion decisively contradicted by evidence from reliable historical sources and numerous archaeological findings.

For example, the Roman emperors Augustus, Claudius, and Tiberius, all mentioned in the New Testament, are factually documented figures in Roman history quite apart from the Bible. No reputable historian would say these emperors existed only in the faith of the New Testament writers. In addition to citing facts concerning the existence of given individuals in the New Testament, there are also numerous persons in the Old Testament that have been verified by historians. In 2014, Lawrence Mykytiuk, an archaeologist at Purdue University, confirmed the historical exis-

137 "More Than a Hobby," *The Economist* (July 2, 2016), 28.

tence of fifty people mentioned in the Hebrew Bible of the Old Testament.[138]

Archaeologists have also confirmed numerous locations and civilizations cited in the Bible that once were dismissed as legendary by Bible critics. In the early 1800s, Bible critics rejected the historical reality of the Sumerian city of Ur, mentioned in Genesis 12, the place from where Abraham hailed, because no extrabiblical publications had ever mentioned Ur. But in the early 1850s, J. E. Taylor discovered the city of Ur under deep layers of sand. Soon additional excavations revealed that this city once had thriving residents, at least by 2000 BC. Its residents used musical instruments, did mathematical calculations, and knew how to write. The latter finding discredited the Bible critics' contention that alphabetical writing did not appear this early in history, an argument they used to contend that Moses (about 1500 BC) could not have written about Abraham in the Book of Genesis.

For many years in the 1800s, Bible critics rejected the Old Testament's references that spoke of the Hittite civilization. They saw these biblical references as nonhistorical, fictional accounts because no extrabiblical publications made mention of Hittites. The references of King Solomon having some Hittite wives and Uriah the Hittite were considered examples of the biblical writers' faith. But in 1906, German archaeologist Hugo Winkler discovered more than ten thousand cuneiform clay tablets in Syria that corroborated the past existence of Hittites there. This discovery de-

138 Lawrence Mykytiuk, "Archaeology Confirms 50 People in the Bible," *Biblical Archaeological Review* (March/April 2014), 42–50.

cisively contradicted the critics' argument that biblical "facts" are only expressions of faith, rather than real history.

Another example is the Pool of Bethesda and its five porches, mentioned in John 5:2–3. The Bible critics dismissed this account as faith-dependent biblical fiction. They argued that pentagonal structures with five porches (porticoes) did not exist in ancient architecture. However, in 1888, archaeologist Conrad Schick discovered this pool with its five porches in Jerusalem. Since then, this ancient pool has been and continues to be visited by tourists from around the globe.

As these examples show, the facts in the Bible are not dependent on faith. Cities cited in the Bible—such as Hebron, Jerusalem, Bethany, Ephesus, Antioch of Syria, and Rome—are facts totally independent of faith. The same is true of other geographical names, such as the Sea of Galilee, the Jordan River, Mount Tabor, the Jezreel Valley, and other sites. Thus, *The Economist* author's assertion that citing "facts" from the Bible "is a statement of faith" is not only false but also reflects an erroneous, idiosyncratic view of faith, not to mention a bias against Christians and the Bible.

"Faith, an End in Itself"

Renowned German theologian Wolfhart Pannenberg has correctly argued that, biblically speaking, *fides quae creditur* (the faith that is believed by Christians) is foundational to the act of believing (*fides qua creditur*). Today, this is reversed. Believing is more important than what is believed. This perceived value of faith as an end in itself was already advocated and expressed two centuries ago by Madame de Staël (1766–1817), a prominent French-Swiss woman of letters:

> I do not know exactly what we must believe, but I believe that we must believe! The eighteenth century did nothing but deny. The human spirit lives by its beliefs. Acquire faith through Christianity, or through German philosophy, or merely through human enthusiasm, but believe in something.[139]

Clearly, Madame de Staël's subjective and idiosyncratic understanding of faith is totally removed from Christianity's unique, exclusive faith.

"Keep the Faith"

Closely related to faith as an end in itself is the idiosyncratic view of faith as having no object. It is frequently expressed by individuals who tell their friends and others to "keep the faith." This clichéd view of faith is at least a century old. In November 1918, Moina Belle Michael, an American public school teacher, happened to read the Canadian poet and soldier surgeon John McCrae's poem "In Flanders Fields" (initially titled "We Shall Not Sleep"). He penned the poem in 1915 to honor the fallen soldiers of World War I buried on the battlefields in Flanders, France, and in neighboring Belgium. She especially liked the poem's first two lines:

> In Flanders fields the poppies blow
> Between the crosses row on row.

139 Cited in Frederick B. Artz, *Reaction and Revolution*, 1814–1832 (New York: Harper & Row, 1934), 49.

These words moved her to introduce the red poppy as a memorial symbol to honor those soldiers who had died in the First World War. Known as "the Poppy Lady," she also scripted five poetic lines in honor of John McCrae's poem. She titled it "We Shall Keep the Faith." These lines read:

> Oh, you who slept in Flanders Fields,
> Sleep sweet—to rise anew!
> We caught the torch you threw
> And holding high, we keep the Faith
> With all who died.[140]

The title is noteworthy, for it talks about faith with no object. Thus, it is a faith entirely unlike Christianity's exclusive faith that has Jesus Christ as its sole and necessary object.

In 1991, almost a hundred years after "the Poppy Lady" wrote "We Shall Keep the Faith," Michael Jackson, Siedah Garrett, and Glen Ballard wrote and released a song titled "Keep the Faith." After twenty-nine stanzas, it has a separate concluding line: "But till that day I said you've got to keep the faith." This song, too, talks about faith with no object.

Conclusion

The above idiosyncratic views of faith are reflections of individuals who evidently have never heard of the faith that was operative among the early Christians as portrayed in the New Testament. Their faith was centered on Christ and exclusively Christian,

140 For a more detailed account see Moina Michael, *The Miracle Flower: The Story of the Flanders Fields Memorial Poppy* (Philadelphia: Dorrance and Company, 1941).

whereas the idiosyncratic views of faith cited in this chapter are the product of the individuals' subjective opinions. None of them reflect even the remotest familiarity with the exclusive faith that was present among the early Christians in the New Testament.

So why are these subjective, idiosyncratic views of faith so commonly cited? Why were they published and thus given some credibility? Perhaps they were published solely because they were voiced by well-known individuals. But perhaps they were also published because there is a void of clear definitions of *faith*; because the concept of faith is frequently mentioned in books, articles, and other contexts without any definition, individuals may feel encouraged to voice their idiosyncratic views to fill the void of undefined faith.

DISCUSSION QUESTIONS

1. Presbyterian theologian J. Gresham Machen once noted that pastors talk about faith but do not say what it is. Given your church experience, how valid is this criticism?
2. If you were asked to give a biblically correct definition of *faith*, how would you define it?
3. Why do we have so many idiosyncratic views of faith?
4. What in our culture contributes to the common perception that believing is more important what is believed?
5. Biblically speaking, what is missing when believing is more important than what is believed?
6. What is missing when we hear people say, "Keep the faith"?
7. When some individuals in well-known publications say that "even talking about 'facts' of the Bible is a statement of faith," why is there usually no rebuttal in sermons, Bible classes, or in church publications?
8. Why is the statement "the Bible is a book of faith" frequently heard but rarely critiqued?

CHAPTER 6

"THE CHRISTIAN FAITH": THE UNRECOGNIZED MISUSE OF FAITH

There is nothing more deceptive than an obvious fact.

Sherlock Holmes, in Arthur Conan Doyle's "The Boscombe Valley Mystery"

Many Christians are accustomed to hearing and saying the appellation "the Christian faith" rather than "the Christian religion" or just "Christianity." So Christians may be surprised by the title of this chapter, which indicates that this appellation is actually a misuse of the New Testament's exclusive use of faith. They are likely surprised by this misuse because there is no evidence in the history of the Church indicating that Christians were ever taught what the appellation "the Christian faith" logically implies, namely, that non-Christian religions also use and value the concept of faith. This implication clashes with the New Testament's teachings that consistently indicate the word *pistis* (faith) and *pistis* language refer only to Christians and never to non-Christians, as documented earlier in chapter 1.

This lack of awareness among Christians harks back to the time when this appellation first appeared in the history of the Church in the latter part of the fourth century. That is when Augustine, renowned Western Church Father, apparently was the first Christian to speak of "the Christian faith." Later, this phrase was used by at least three other prominent Christian leaders: the Venerable Bede in the 700s, Nicholas of Cusa in the 1400s, and Martin Luther in the 1500s.[141]

To aid in understanding the importance and the relevancy of the present chapter's discussion pertaining to the appellation "the Christian faith," this chapter first provides a brief history of where, when, and how the name *Christians* first appeared in the history of the Church. It also documents where, when, and how the name *Christianity* appeared. *Christianity* is a biblically compatible appellation that appeared in the first decade of the second century AD, several centuries before the appellation "the Christian faith."

The Earliest Names of Christ's Followers

When the dispersed followers of Jesus Christ (mostly Hellenistic Jews) fled Jerusalem and Galilee after the stoning of Stephen, the first Christian martyr in AD 35/36, they went to Phoenicia, Cyprus, and Antioch in Syria, according to Acts 11:19. Their presence—especially at Antioch, one of the larger and more prosperous cities in the Roman Empire—soon became noteworthy, even though they did not have only one distinctive name. They were known as "disciples," "brethren," "saints," "Nazarenes," and "the Way."

141 It is possible there were some other Church leaders in the Middle Ages who also used "the Christian faith" appellation, for I did not make a special effort to see whether there were others.

Before the apostle Paul's conversion, when he was hunting and persecuting followers of Christ, he asked the high priest in Jerusalem to reveal names of men and women in the synagogues of Damascus who were members of "the Way." He wanted to bring some of them bound to Jerusalem (Acts 9:1–2). Years later, after his conversion, Paul told the pagan residents at Ephesus that their molten-silver images of gods were not gods. This criticism prompted a major social disturbance in the city's stadium that blamed followers of "the Way" (Acts 19:23).

The appellation "the Way" referred to those who sought to heed and observe Christ's teachings. Jesus had told His disciple Thomas, "I am *the way*, and the truth, and the life. No one comes to the Father except through Me" (John 14:6, emphasis added). From these words, it is reasonable to assume that "the Way" became a shorthand label for what Christ's followers spiritually believed in word and deed. This conclusion finds support from the Book of Acts, where we read that a certain Jew in Ephesus named Apollos was "instructed in *the way* of the Lord" (Acts 18:25, emphasis added). The name "the Way" also denoted the path to be traveled and the life to be lived, as followers of Christ in a Christless world.

The Name *Christian* First Heard at Antioch

According to Acts 11:26, Christ's followers first heard some residents of Antioch in Syria referring to them as "Christians" (*Christianoi*) in the early 40s. Various scholars have speculated concerning the name's origin. Several possibilities have been cited. Because the name *Christianoi* is a Greek name with a Latin suffix (thus a hybrid name), some think that Antioch's Greek inhabitants coined the word, while others, because of the Latin ending, think it might have been the Romans. That the Jews introduced the name is not likely, for that would have indicated they had accepted Jesus as the Messiah (the Christ). Various scholars have noted that there is no evidence, or even a hint, that Christians themselves chose the name. Although the name *Christians* is biblically compatible, some historians have suggested that the name was not intended to commend their movement.

Following Acts 11:26, the name *Christian* appears only two more times in the New Testament, in Acts 26:28 and in 1 Peter 4:16. In the latter reference, the name appears to reflect the connotation of cultural contempt. This prompted the apostle Peter to urge the recipients of his letter to "not be ashamed, but to glorify God in that *name*" (emphasis added). Peter's noting that the name *Christian* was viewed with contempt by the pagan Romans appears to be the first recorded instance (in the early 60s) of the name's negative perception. Then, about fifty years later, the Roman historian Cornelius Tacitus, who despised Christians, wrote that *Christianoi* (Christians) was a "vulgar appellation."[142]

The negative view of Christ's followers is also mentioned in the second century by some Early Church Fathers, who reported numerous accounts in which the name *Christian* was viewed negatively and in which those identified with the name were persecuted and sometimes executed. Justin Martyr, an early Christian apologist martyred under the Roman Emperor Marcus Aurelius, revealed nu-

142 Cornelius Tacitus, *Annuals* 15:44.

merous instances of martyrdom in his book *The First Apology of Justin*. It notes Christians being persecuted simply for bearing the name *Christian*. In this book, he criticizes the Roman authorities by saying, "If anyone acknowledges that he is a Christian, you [Romans] punish him on account of his acknowledgement."[143]

Regarding the origin of the name *Christian*, the followers of Christ at Antioch had become quite numerous, composed of Gentiles and Hellenistic Jews. Here, they had grown as a community distinct from Judaism, and thus the Antiochians named them "Christians." That they, as followers of Christ, received this name was evidently a logical consequence of their behavior, as one scholar explains it.

> They delighted to tell of His [Christ's] mighty miracles, of His holy life, of the extraordinary circumstances which accompanied His death, and of His resurrection and ascension. . . . When they prayed, they prayed to Christ; when they sang, they sang praise to Christ; when they preached, they preached Christ. Well then might the heathen multitude agree with one voice to call them Christians.[144]

The pagan multitudes at Antioch may indeed have chosen the name *Christian* to express their contempt, consistent with the name's early connotation, as noted by the apostle Peter: "If anyone suffers as a Christian, let him not be ashamed, but let him glori-

143 Justin Martyr, *The First Apology of Justin in Ante-Nicene Christian Library, Translations of the Fathers*, eds. Alexander Roberts and James Donaldson (Edinburgh: T and T Clark, 1857), 10.

144 W. D. Killen, *The Ancient Church: Its History, Doctrine, Worship, and Constitution, Traced for the First Three Hundred Years* (New York: Anson D. F. Randolph and Company, 1883), 57.

fy God in that name" (1 Peter 4:16). That Christ's followers experienced contempt has merit. For when Paul testified before King Agrippa, reminding him of Christ's death and resurrection, the king responded, "In a short time would you persuade me to be a Christian?" (Acts 26:28). The context of Agrippa's use of the name *Christian* appears to reflect contempt.

In addition to Christ's followers receiving the name *Christian* at Antioch, several other important occurrences originated there. It was Antioch, not Jerusalem, that became the cradle of Christianity. It was Antioch from which the apostle Paul launched his three missionary journeys. Here Paul rebuked Peter for siding with the Judaizers who taught that circumcision was necessary for church membership (see Galatians 2:11–12). Here Paul's action opened the door for admitting the uncircumcised Gentiles as members of the Church (see Acts 11:19–26). And it was here, at Antioch, that the episcopal form of ecclesiastical government became part of the Early Church's organizational structure near the end of the first century.[145]

The Name *Christian* Not Used by the Apostle Paul

Paul's three missionary journeys began at Antioch in the decade of the 40s. He certainly must have heard and known that his fellow followers of Christ were called Christians at Antioch, where he and Barnabas had faithfully ministered and taught "for a whole year" (Acts 11:26). And as just noted, we know heard the name

145 Glanville Downey, *A History of Antioch in Syria from Seleucus to the Arab Conquest* (Princeton, NJ: Princeton University Press, 1961), 282.

Christian when he testified before King Agrippa a decade or so later.

But Paul never used the name *Christian* or *Christians* in any of his epistles in the New Testament that he wrote during a period of about fifteen years after having left Antioch in the late 40s. And although Peter (in AD 63 or 64) used the name *Christian* in 1 Peter 4:16, the three epistles of John do not. The epistles Hebrews, James, Jude, 2 Peter, and Revelation, all written at least a decade after the name *Christian* first appeared at Antioch, also do not use this name. The name's absence in these epistles is somewhat curious, given that the early followers of Christ were favorably called "the Way" and sometimes "disciples," "saints," and "Nazarenes." The new name *Christians* was more slowly adopted, even though the name "Christians [*Christianoi*] made it clear that they were agents and representatives of the Messiah."[146]

Paul's epistles certainly underscored Jesus as the Christ (Messiah). No scholar of the New Testament would deny this. So why did he not use the name *Christians*? Here it is interesting to note a particular passage Paul wrote in his Epistle to the Galatians: "So then, as we have opportunity, let us do good to everyone, and especially to those who are of the household of faith" (6:10). In place of "the household of faith," he could have written "the household of Christians" with the same force and effectiveness. Moreover, several times (Romans 3:22; 4:11; 1 Corinthians 1:21; 14:22), he called Christ's followers "the believers" (*oi pisteuontes*), whom in these passages he could also have called "Christians." Why he chose not

146 Elias J. Bickerman, "The Name of Christians," *Harvard Theological Review* (April 1949), 123.

to call them Christians remains unknown, but this question apparently has not intrigued New Testament scholars.

The Name *Christian* in Early Christian Writings

The *Didache*, an early church manual, began circulating in the Early Church in about AD 100.[147] In this document's various instructions, the Early Church's members are told "that no idle Christian [*Christianos*] is to live among you."[148] Thus, the *Didache* marks the first known instance that the name *Christian* appeared in written form after its three appearances in the New Testament.

Like the apostle Paul, some of the Apostolic Fathers[149] did not use the name *Christian* or *Christians*. For example, Clement of Rome (AD 35–99) did not use the name *Christians* in his epistles. Neither did the author of *The Epistle of Barnabas* in about 130. Why neither of these books used the name *Christians* we do not know. On the other hand, Bishop Ignatius of Antioch (c. 35–c. 108),[150] a contemporary of Clement of Rome, did use the name *Christian*. Ignatius penned several brief letters on his journey from Antioch to Rome, where he expected to be executed as a martyr for Christ under the reign of Emperor Trajan. One letter is titled "To the Magnesians," written to the Church in Magnesia near Ephesus. In this letter, Ignatius used the name *Christians* (*Christianoi*), and

147 The date of the *Didache*'s origin has not been firmly established, but many scholars say the date of AD 100 is reasonably probable, even though some opt for a date in the first or second decade of the second century.

148 *Didache* in *The Apostolic Fathers*, ed. and trans. Bart Ehrman (Cambridge, MA: Harvard University Press, 2003), 437.

149 The Apostolic Fathers were Christian authors in the first half of the second century who had personally interacted with some of Christ's twelve apostles

150 Some scholars cite the date of 108 for Ignatius's martyrdom, and some cite a date of several years later.

in this same letter, he is the first known follower of Christ to use the name *Christianity* (*Christianismos*).[151] On this same journey, he also penned "To the Philadelphians," in which he again used the name *Christianity* (*Christianismos*).[152] The names *Christian* (*Christianos*) and *Christianity* (*Christianismos*) also appear fifty years later in the document *Martyrdom of Polycarp*, written shortly after the pagan Romans executed Polycarp, bishop of Smyrna, in 156.[153]

By the latter half of the second century, the names *Christians* and *Christianity* had gained full acceptance. Both names appear in the writings of numerous Christian authors from this time. Irenaeus, bishop of Lyons in Gaul (now modern France), likely martyred in 202, wrote about "Christian catechumens" in his *Fragments.* In the same document, he made the interesting statement "The business of the *Christian* is nothing else than to be ever preparing for death" (emphasis added). Justin Martyr (cited in another context above) penned several apologetical treatises. His longest work, *Dialogue with Trypho, a Jew*, mentions the names *Christian* and *Christians* numerous times. Athenagoras (133–90), a prominent Christian apologist, used the name *Christian* frequently in his treatise *A Plea for the Christians*, in which he addressed Emperor Marcus Aurelius to treat the persecuted Christians with justice.

By the third century, the names *Christian* and *Christianity* were used by virtually every noteworthy Christian author. One

---

151 Ignatius, *To the Magnesians, The Apostolic Fathers: Greek Texts and English Translations*, ed. Michael W. Holmes (Grand Rapids: Baker Book House, 1999), 152, 156.

152 Ignatius, *To the Philadelphians, The Apostolic Fathers: Greek Texts and English Translations*, ed. Michael W. Holmes (Grand Rapids: Baker Book House, 1999), 178.

153 *Martyrdom of Polycarp, Bishop of Smyrna*, ed. Bart D. Ehrman, *The Apostolic Fathers* (Cambridge, MA: Harvard University Press, 2003), 380.

of the more prominent Church Fathers in the third century who used these two names was Clement of Alexandria (d. c. 215). He taught at the renowned Catechetical School in Alexandria, and he spoke about "the life of Christians" in his work *The Instructor.* The Latin Church Father Tertullian (d. c. 225), an ardent defender of Christianity in northern Africa, used the names *Christians* and *Christianity* copiously. The Church Father Origen (d. c. 253) wrote the lengthy, brilliant critique *Contra Celsus*, which countered the pagan Celsus's attacks on Jesus' teachings and the New Testament. Origen used the words *Christian* and *Christianity* throughout this classic document. Cyprian (200–58), who served as a bishop at Carthage, wrote several epistles in which the word *Christian* appears numerous times.

Given the frequent appearance of the names *Christian* and *Christianity* by the third century, there is no need to cite additional theological documents to show that these two names continued to permeate the pages of the Church's theological literature. Whatever reluctance there might have been on the part of some early Christian writers to use the name *Christian* was no longer a concern. Thus, the names *Christian* and *Christianity* continue to appear on hundreds and hundreds of pages and in titles of books and articles to the present day.

Although the names *Christian* and *Christianity* from the second century on appear in numerous theological epistles and treatises by Christian writers in the Early Church, there is an interesting exception worth noting. It is found in one of the epistles by the Church Father Augustine (354–430), bishop of Hippo in northern Africa. He reports that some followers of Christ in his time still called themselves Jews rather than Christians.[154] This report is reminiscent of what appears in the Book of Revelation, where its author in 2:9 and 3:9 uses the Greek word *Ioudaious* (Jews) for the followers of Christ. Thus, as Shaye J. D. Cohen has noted, "The author of Revelation believes that the title 'Jew' (*Ioudaios*) is an honorable designation and properly belongs to those who believe in Christ."[155] The author saw these believers in Christ as Jews, not because they were circumcised outwardly in the flesh, but because they were circumcised inwardly in the heart through faith. These were the real Jews, as Paul had similarly told the Christians in Rome: "For no one is a Jew who is merely one outwardly, nor is circumcision outward and physical. But a Jew is one inwardly, and circumcision is a matter of the heart, by the Spirit, not by the letter" (Romans 2:28–29).

It is interesting indeed that the writer of the Book of Revelation still used "*Ioudaious*" (Jews) rather than "Christians" some fifty years after the name *Christians* was first uttered at Antioch in the early 40s. It is hard to imagine that by this time the author of Revelation had not heard that his fellow followers of Christ in some locations were called Christians in honor of Christ. Thus, did this author of Revelation have some reluctance to use the name *Christians*, and if so, was his reluctance perhaps akin to Paul's? Of course, we do not know.

---

154 Augustine, Epistle 196, *Corpus Scriptorum Ecclesiasticorum Latinorum* (1911), 57:216–30.

155 Shaye J. D. Cohen, "'Those Who Say They are Jews and Are Not': 'How Do You Know a Jew in Antiquity When You See One?'" in Shaye J. D. Cohen and Ernest S. Frerichs, eds., *Diasporas in Antiquity* (Atlanta: Scholars Press, 1993), 2. I am indebted to Cohen for his reference to Augustine.

"The Christian Faith" Not in the New Testament

Although the word *Christian* appears in the New Testament three times, the word *Christianity*, as we have seen, is a post–New Testament word from the first decade of the second century. What today we call "Christianity," the New Testament simply calls "the faith" (*he pistis*), as in Romans 1:8. The evangelist Luke in Acts 13:8, for instance, wrote of a sorcerer attempting to turn a given proconsul (a Christian) away from "the faith" (*tns pisteos*). Below we will see some examples of Paul's writings that speak of Christianity as "the faith."

That the phrase "the Christian faith" is not found in the New Testament but is now common and widespread prompts an important question: Was the individual who first spoke of "the Christian faith" aware of what this phrase implied—namely, that faith was not exclusively Christian and that non-Christians also had and valued faith?

According to Wilfred Cantwell Smith, "pre-modern Christian writers appear not to have thought explicitly of 'Christian faith' because they were unaware of any other kind. They thought of faith absolutely, as something that had become available to mankind only, or virtually only, through Christ and the Church."[156] Smith added, "In Catholic thought, it is my impression that throughout the Middle Ages the dominant custom was for the concept *fides* [faith] to be used without specification."[157] Thus, Christians apparently did not consider *fides* applicable to non-Christian religions.

156 Wilfred Cantwell Smith, *Belief and History* (Charlottesville: University Press of Virginia, 1977), 125.

157 Ibid.

However, as just quoted, Smith also said it is his "impression" and it was "the dominant custom" that *fides* in the Middle Ages was "used without specification." This is not a strong, affirmative statement. And, as we shall see below, it is also not quite correct.

More recently, Smith, contrary to his statements just quoted, has cited Peter Abelard's book *Theologia christiana* (Christian Theology), published circa 1134, as being "the only instance before the nineteenth century where such a qualification [of faith] is enshrined in a title."[158] By his saying "before the nineteenth century," Smith has in mind Friedrich Schleiermacher's book *Der christliche Glaube* (The Christian Faith),[159] published in 1821/22. This book, published seven hundred years after Abelard's book, clearly ascribes faith to non-Christian religions. Smith even says Abelard was Schleiermacher's "sole predecessor"[160] in this use of faith.

First Appearance of "*Christiana Fides*" (The Christian Faith)[161]

Contrary to Smith's earlier statements, Augustine did speak of "the Christian faith" in some of his writings, as noted above. He did so in his classic work, *Confessions*, written in the latter part of the decade in the 390s. He mentions "the authority of the Christian faith all over the world" (*auctoritatis christianae fidei toto orbe*; VI 11 19). In *Confessions* VII 19 25, he wrote about his friend Alypius having "moved more slowly toward the Christian faith" (*ad ipsam*

---

158 Wilfred Cantwell Smith, "On Mistranslations of Book Titles," *Religious Studies* (March 1984), 36.

159 The original title of Schleiermacher's book in German was *Der christliche Glaube nach den Grundsätzen der evangelische Kirche in Zusammenhange dargestellt* (1821/22).

160 Smith, "On Mistranslations of Book Titles," 36.

161 As readers may know, in Latin the phrase "*Christiana fides*" (the Christian faith) does not have the definite article as in English.

christianam fidem pigrius movebatur).[162] In still another work, he wrote about some individuals "converting to the Christian faith" (*conuersum ad Christianam fidem*).[163]

Though Augustine spoke of "the Christian faith," he does not seem to have explicitly ascribed faith to non-Christian religions. But by using the phrase "the Christian faith," he nevertheless implied that non-Christian religions also had faith.

Regarding Augustine's use of "the Christian faith," it is important to note some of the important Church Fathers who preceded him but did not use this appellation: Ignatius of Antioch (d. c. 108), Polycarp of Smyrna (d. 155), Justin Martyr (d. 165), Theophilus of Antioch (d. 181), Athenagoras of Athens (d. 190), Irenaeus (d. 202), Tertullian (d. c. 225), Hippolytus (d. c. 236), Minucius Felix (d. c. 250), Cyprian (d. 258), Lactantius (d. 320), Methodius (d. 312), and Arnobius (d. 330). They all published noteworthy treatises that greatly aided and helped sustain the early Christians during the trying times of some severe persecutions. Their writings over a period of three centuries contain the words *Christian* and *Christians* and sometimes also the word *Christianity*. But not one of their writings ever spoke of "the Christian faith."

Hence, it appears that Augustine is the first known Christian who wrote of "the Christian faith." This, of course, raises the question as to what motivated him to use this appellation, given that it

162 The citations from Augustine's *Confessions* are found in *Augustine's Confessions*, Books 1–8, edited and translated by Carolyn J. B. Hammond (Cambridge, MA: Harvard University Press, 2014), 276, 277 and 344, 345, respectively.

163 Augustine, *Corpus Scriptorum Ecclesiasticorum Latinorum*, Epistularum XCIII (Prague: F. Tempsky, 1898), 34:495. Augustine published numerous works. And given that I have not researched everything he has written, it is possible that he may also have used the phrase "the Christian faith" in some of those writings.

implies faith is not exclusively Christian, an implication that conflicts with the New Testament's use of *pistis* (faith), as noted earlier. For as we saw in chapter 1, according to Teresa Morgan, the "New Testament writers never use *pistis* language to refer to anyone other than Christians."[164] Thus, did Augustine not know this noteworthy fact from his knowledge of the New Testament?

Why did Augustine, proficient in Latin, not simply say "*Christianismus*" (Christianity)? This question is relevant because by his time the name *Christianity* had been widely used for three centuries by numerous Church Fathers, as shown above. The name *Christianity*, coined by Ignatius in the first decade of the second century, is fully compatible with the New Testament's use of faith as Christianity's exclusive concept, but Augustine's use of "*Christianae fidei*" (Christian faith) is not compatible, according to the New Testament.

Three hundred years after Augustine, the Venerable Bede (672–735), a British monk of the Benedictine Order, in 731 published his noteworthy *Ecclesiastical History of the English People* in Latin. In this book of three hundred pages, Bede, like Augustine, sometimes also wrote of "the Christian faith" (*Christianae fidei*) and "the Christian religion" (*Christianae religionis*).[165] But he seemed to prefer saying "*Christianae fidei*." On one occasion, he urged that church customs should conform to those used by "the Church and the Christian faith" (*ecclesiasticam et Christianae fidei*).[166] As with Augustine, we do not know whether Bede realized that by using

164 Teresa Morgan, *Roman Faith and Christian Faith* (Oxford: Oxford University Press, 2015), 235.

165 Bertram Colgrave and R. A. B. Mynors, eds., *Bede's Ecclesiastical History of the English People* (Oxford: Clarendon Press, 1969), 72

166 Ibid., 546.

the appellation "the Christian faith" he was in effect saying that *pistis* (faith) was not exclusively Christian. And why did he, proficient in Latin, not simply write *Christianismus* (Christianity)?

Then, in the fifteenth century, Christian philosopher and German cardinal Nicholas of Cusa (1401–64) published his book *Cribratio Alkorani* (A Scrutiny of the Koran) in defense of Christianity. In this volume, he wrote, "From the beginning of the Christian faith" (*et cum ab initio fidei christianae*).[167] One wonders why he did not simply say, "From the beginning of Christianity."

Next, nearly a century after Nicholas of Cusa, we find Martin Luther (1483–1546) writing of "the Christian faith" (*der Christliche Glaube*) in his treatise *The Estate of Marriage*.[168] On another occasion, lamenting the attacks that Christians often suffered at the hands of the Islamic Turks, he called them "the enemy of the Christian faith" (*der feind den Christlichen Glaubens*).[169] And in his *Ordinance of a Common Chest*, he contended that monasticism was incompatible with "our Christian faith" (*unser Christlicher Glaube*).[170]

The phrase "the Christian faith" implies that Christianity is not the only religion with the concept of faith, an implication that has not gone unrecognized. Martin Luther, for example, recognized this implication in his treatise *On War against the Turk*, where

167 *Cribratio Alkorani* in *Nikolas von Kues Werke*, Band II (Berlin: Walter De Gruyter and Company, 1967), 445–46.

168 Martin Luther, "*Vom ehelichen Leben*," *D. Martin Luthers Werke* (Weimar: Hermann Böhlaus Nachfolger, 1907), 10, part 2, 292.

169 Martin Luther, "*Vom Kriege widder die Turken*," *D. Martin Luthers Werke* (Weimar: Hermann Böhlaus Nachfolger, 1909), 30, part 2, 132.

170 Martin Luther, "*Ordenung eyns gemynen kastens*," *D. Martin Luthers Werke* (Weimar Hermann Böhlaus Nachfolger, 1891), 12:17.

he refers to Turkish religion as "the Turkish faith" (*der Turkissche Glaube*). Apparently, his writing of "the Turkish faith" was prompted, perhaps spontaneously, by his having previously written of "*der Christliche Glaube*" (the Christian faith) in other contexts. And as with Augustine, Bede, and Nicholas of Cusa, why did Luther not simply use the word *Christianity*—"*Christianismus*" in Latin or "*Christentum*" in German?

We do not know why Augustine chose to write of "the Christian faith." Nor do we know why Bede did as Augustine did. But given Augustine's wide, prominent influence in the Church at large from the fifth century and after, it is plausible to assume that Bede, three hundred years later, may have been influenced by Augustine's usage. Thus, he also wrote of "the Christian faith," likely not realizing what the appellation implied with respect to non-Christian religions. The influence of Augustine may also explain why Nicholas of Cusa, a thousand years later, wrote of "the Christian faith." And Luther, a former Augustinian friar, may also have unthinkingly reflected Augustine's influence when he, too, wrote of "*der Christliche Glaube*" (the Christian faith).

When these four theologians spoke of "the Christian faith," they likely did not envision how this appellation would result in non-Christians appending the word *faith* to their religion's formal name, thereby hijacking the New Testament's exclusive faith of Christians. History shows this hijacking has indeed taken place, for we now hear and read of "the Buddhist faith," "the Islamic faith," "the Hindu faith," "the Mormon faith," and so on.

Given that Augustine, Bede, Nicholas of Cusa, and Luther

wrote and preached about the role of faith in the life of Christians, there is one possibility that may shed some light on why they spoke of "the Christian faith," implying that non-Christian religions also had faith. Though they certainly knew that *pistis* meant "faith," they apparently did not know it was the New Testament that first used the Greek word *pistis* as a religious principle, previously unknown to the Greeks, which made *pistis* exclusively Christian. Thus, they may not have realized that using the appellation "the Christian faith" clashed with the New Testament's exclusively Christian use of *pistis*. Here it is helpful to note that these two aspects of *pistis* (as a religious principle and its Christian exclusiveness), discussed in greater length in chapter 1, evidently were not known by Christians before William Henry Paine Hatch in 1917 first made known these two aspects of *pistis* in the New Testament. Thus, these four churchmen, born centuries before 1917, apparently did not know of these two characteristics of *pistis* when they read and studied the New Testament's twenty-seven books. They apparently did not consciously perceive that *pistis* and *pistis* language in the New Testament are only used with respect to Christians.

Moreover, if Augustine, Bede, Nicholas, and Luther in studying the New Testament used commentaries, it would not necessarily have helped them. For commentaries often fail to note certain theological distinctiveness of some biblically important concepts. If their biblical commentaries did not indicate that *pistis* language was exclusively Christian, it would not have been unusual. Here it is fitting to cite the renowned *Theological Dictionary of the New Testament* (1969). It contains a long scholarly survey of fifty-four pages devoted to *pistis* and its different verbal forms, but it makes no mention that *pistis* language in the New Testament consistently refers only to Christians. This omission is no exception, for today's New Testament commentaries similarly say nothing about *pistis* and *pistis* language being exclusively Christian. It just does not seem to be consciously noticed. Thus, countless Christians, including their pastors and theologians, to the present day do not seem to know this vitally significant fact regarding *pistis* in the New Testament. Not knowing this biblical truth has prevented them from realizing that when they use the appellation "the Christian faith," it clashes with the exclusively Christian nature and role of *pistis* and *pistis* language in the New Testament.

Why Not "The Faith" (*He Pistis*)?

When Augustine, Bede, Nicholas of Cusa, and Luther spoke of "the Christian faith," one wonders why they did not speak or write of "the faith" (*he pistis*), as the New Testament sometimes does when it refers to Christianity or to its teachings. In Luke 18:8, for example, Jesus spoke of faith in that sense when He wondered whether He would find "the faith" (*ten pistin*) on earth when He returns at the end of time. This objective sense of faith was also what the apostle Paul spoke of in Galatians 1:23, when he referred to himself as the one who preaches "the faith" (*ten pistin*). Paul also wrote about some who would "depart from the faith" (*tines tns pisteos*; 1 Timothy 4:1).

Interestingly, "the faith" in the Greek New Testament occurs in all four grammatical cases: nominative, genitive, dative, and accusative. This unique reality did not escape the early Christians after the apostles had completed writing the New Testament. Thus, Irenaeus, bishop of Lyons (c. 130–202), the Early Church's opponent of Gnosticism and famed author of *Adversus Haereses* (Against Heresies), referred to Christianity as "*he pistis*" (the faith). Similarly, after the Council of Nicaea in AD 325, many Christians referred to the Nicene Creed as "symbol of the faith" (*symbolon tns pisteos*). And Eusebius of Caesarea (d. c. 339) referred to Christians as being of "the faith" (*tns pisteos*) in his renowned *Historia Ecclesiastica* (Church History).

When Christians speak of "the faith" or "symbol of the faith," they reflect the words of Christ, the apostle Paul, and some early Christians in the post–New Testament era. The phrase "the faith" reinforces the New Testament's use of faith as Christianity's exclusive concept. And unlike the appellation "the Christian faith," to say "the faith" does not imply that faith is not exclusively Christian. Hence, one wonders why in the history of the Church the biblical appellation "the faith" did not prevail but lost to the contrabiblical appellation "the Christian faith."

How "The Christian Faith" Appellation Became Popular

Although the phrase "the Christian faith" was occasionally used by Augustine, Bede, Nicholas of Cusa, and Luther, there appears to be no evidence throughout the Middle Ages that this appellation had become a widely accepted part of the Church's theological vocabulary. Thus, the widespread use of "the Christian faith," now spoken by many Christians, primarily appears to be the product of

Friedrich Schleiermacher's book *Der christliche Glaube* (The Christian Faith). The title of this book and its distinctly ascribing faith to all religions served to popularize the phrase "the Christian faith." But it took a hundred years or so, to about the second decade of the twentieth century, for authors of articles and books to use this appellation with increasing frequency. This helped make it theologically and culturally acceptable as people heard it spoken and saw it in print, aided by no objections from any Christian theologians who had never asked whether it was biblically appropriate for Christians to speak of "the Christian faith." The culture's "cake of custom" had effectively barred that question.[171]

"The Christian Faith"
Appellation Not Unanimously Used

Although Augustine, Bede, Nicholas of Cusa, and Luther spoke of "the Christian faith," numerous Christian authors after their time did not use this appellation. Instead, they wrote of "Christianity" or "the Christian religion." The following are a few examples.

In 1536, John Calvin (1509–64) published his well-known theological work *Christianae Religionis Institutio* (Institutes of the Christian Religion). He did not use the phrase "the Christian faith" in the book's title. One century later, the Westminster Confession (1647) in England spoke of "the Christian religion" in its doctrinal formulations, and it also spoke of "Christianity," but it did not say "the Christian faith."

Across the ocean, in America, George Whitefield (1714–70),

171 Walter Bagehot (1826–77), British journalist, used the concept "cake of custom" to explain the role of culture in preventing people from examining cultural customs.

known for his role in the Great Awakening, preached numerous sermons that reportedly even enthralled the deist Benjamin Franklin. Thousands gathered to hear Whitefield preach. He often made references to "Christianity," but "the Christian faith" does not appear in his sermons. Similarly, Jonathan Edwards (1703–58), also an active participant in the Great Awakening, only spoke of "Christianity" and "Christian religion" in his sermons."[172] Another noteworthy American example is Timothy Dwight (1752–1817), sermonizer and a president of Yale College, who in one of his sermons spoke of "Christianity" and "the Christian religion." But the phrase "the Christian faith" was not heard from him.[173]

In the early years of the United States' political formation, some of its founding fathers were not shy to voice their conviction that their young nation's founding documents reflected the values of "the Christian religion." Thus, John Adams (1735–1826), foreign diplomat, signer of the country's Constitution, and second president of the country, stated that the American government is "grounded on reason, morality, and the Christian religion."[174] Similarly, James Madison (1751–1836), one of the authors of *The Federalist Papers* and the country's fourth president, in his "Memorial and Remonstrance" document (1785) spoke of "the Christian religion."[175] Neither Adams nor Madison spoke of "the Christian faith."

172 *The Sermons of Jonathan Edwards: A Reader*, eds. Wilson H. Kimnach, Kenneth P. Minkema, Douglas A. Sweeny (New Haven: Yale University Press, 1999).

173 Timothy Dwight, *Sermons* (New Haven: Hezekiah Howe and Durrie and Peck, 1828), vol. 2. This book contains thirty-two sermons.

174 C. F. Adams, ed., *The Works of John Adams* (Boston: C. Little and James Brown, 1851), 4:293.

175 James Madison, "Memorial and Remonstrance," in *The Papers of James Madison*, ed. Robert A. Rut-

In the latter half of the nineteenth century, American preacher and social activist Henry Ward Beecher (1813–87) preached lengthy sermons advocating abolition of slavery. One of his sermons, "The Spread of Christian Manhood in America," mentioned "Christianity" nineteen times, but the phrase "the Christian faith" is absent.[176] Similarly, American evangelist Dwight L. Moody (1837–99), in a volume of eighty-three sermons and twenty-nine public addresses, frequently spoke of "Christianity" but never of "the Christian faith."[177] And in a more scholarly vein, George Park Fisher (1827–1909), once professor of divinity at Yale College, published *The Supernatural Origin of Christianity* (1870) and *The Christian Religion* (1886). He, too, did not speak of "the Christian faith."

Although some authors still speak of "Christianity" or "the Christian religion," both options are now seen less and less frequently in print. "The Christian faith" appellation is now profusely prominent when Christianity is the topic in books, articles, and even sermons. When Christians speak of "the Christian faith," as so many do, they are unwittingly and unintentionally denying the exclusive faith of Christians, which is unequivocally taught in the New Testament.

Conclusion

Christians have for centuries heard the appellation "the Christian faith" spoken in sermons, Bible classes, and casual conversa-

land, et. al. (Chicago: University of Chicago Press, 1973), 8:301.

176 Henry Ward Beecher, *The Sermons of Henry Ward Beecher* (New York: J. B. Ford and Company, 1874), 23–37.

177 Dwight L. Moody, *New Sermons, Addresses, and Prayers* (New York: Henry S. Goodspeed and Company, 1877).

tions. They have also seen it in various religious and secular publications. And they themselves have been using the phrase "the Christian faith" when speaking or writing. But having now learned from the present chapter that this phrase conflicts with the New Testament's exclusively Christian role and nature of faith, they are undoubtedly surprised, and rightly so. For as noted earlier, there is no evidence in the history of the Church that Christians were ever taught by church leaders or theologians that *pistis* (faith) is an exclusively Christian concept. Thus, when they spoke of "the Christian faith," they unknowingly implied that Christianity was not the only religion that valued faith. The historical absence of any Christian objection for Christians using this appellation is truly enigmatic. Why had no Christian leader ever called attention to this important faith-related anomaly?

One can only surmise that the Church's leaders did not realize or know that the phrase "the Christian faith" clashes with the New Testament's portrayal of faith as being exclusively Christian. That they did not seem to consciously notice that *pistis* and *pistis* language never refer to anyone other than Christians in the New Testament can perhaps be charitably explained. For when they read the twenty-seven books of the New Testament, they did not consciously perceive that *pistis* was exclusively Christian. This oversight, to some degree, can be understood given that the New Testament (as noted in chapter 1) does not have a declarative sentence stating this unique role and nature of *pistis* (faith). To perceive this fact regarding *pistis* requires the readers' discerning perception, which they apparently failed to perceive. Thus, the Church's leaders never taught the Christian populace that their God-given faith (*pistis*) was an exclusive phenomenon found present and active only in the New Testament's Christian fellowship.

Some Christians may think that if they were to accent "*the* Christian faith," it would solve the problem, and so they could retain this appellation, but it would not. Accenting the definite article makes the appellation's implied faith of non-Christian religions only seem less valid or less important. The implication that non-Christian religions also have faith, however, remains unchanged. Also, when Christians say "the Christian faith," it easily prompts them, rather spontaneously, to refer to non-Christian groups as faiths as well, such as "the Mormon faith," "the Muslim faith," "the Buddhist faith," and so on. These non-Christian appellations are the spontaneous effects that result from well-meaning Christians having frequently heard and used the phrase "the Christian faith."

Here it seems relevant to note that the spontaneous effect appears to have occurred in Martin Luther's publications. As indicated above, he used the phrase "the Christian faith" (*der Christliche Glaube*) in some of his writings. In his treatise *On War against the Turk*, he referred to the religion of the Turks as "the Turkish faith" (*der Turkissche Glaube*).[178] Another time, he spoke of the Turks having an "invented faith."[179] Thus, it appears that his speaking of "the Turkish faith" was the spontaneous effect prompted by his previous writing and speaking of "the Christian faith."

178 Martin Luther, "*Vom Kriege der die Turken*," *D. Martin Luthers Werke* (Weimar: Hermann Böhlaus Nachfolger, 1909), 30, part 2, 132.

179 Martin Luther, "Lectures on Genesis, Chapters 21–25," *Luther's Works*, eds. Jaroslav Pelikan and Walter Hansen (St. Louis: Concordia Publishing House, 1964), 4:124.

In chapter 3, we saw that the West's now multiculturalist-oriented culture has acculturated Christians to speak of *faith* and *religion* as synonyms. The word *faith* or *faiths* is used when they mean *religion* or *religions*, even though the synonymizing of *faith* and *religion* conflicts with the New Testament's exclusive use of faith. Thus, conscientious Christians are urged to stop using *faith* as a synonym for *religion*, whether in the singular or plural sense. Similarly, they also need to cease using the appellation "the Christian faith."

It is also important to note that when Christians use the appellation "the Christian faith," they make the word *Christian* an adjective. This is another way of implying Christianity is just another religion along with others that value faith, and hence the faith of Christians is not seen or known as exclusive. Perhaps Christians who now know that this appellation, although familiar and popular, is at odds with the New Testament may be consciously motivated to stop saying it.

But they may unfortunately continue to speak of "the Christian faith," contrary to the New Testament, because most people, and Christians are no exception, find it difficult to depart from their culture's verbal expressions once they have personally adopted them. As the Latin poet Ovid stated, "Nothing is more powerful than custom or habit." Moreover, this appellation is ubiquitous in books and articles that discuss Christianity, a custom that will further make it difficult for concerned Christians consistently to say "Christianity" rather than "the Christian faith." But if they were to do so, they would be underscoring the New Testament's use of *pis-*

tis as exclusively and uniquely Christian. This is what today's secular world needs to hear at a time when all non-Christian religions in the West's syncretistic culture are widely and erroneously seen as having faith and truth value akin to Christianity. Briefly stated, Christianity needs its members to be self-consciously distinct from their culture.

Finally, if Christians were consistently to speak and write of "Christianity" rather than "the Christian faith," they would also be reaffirming the historical evidence, now essentially unknown to many Christians and non-Christians, that the religious meaning of *faith* has never been an indigenous concept of any non-Christian religion before *faith* (*pistis*) first became known and used in the New Testament. As Dieter Lührmann has correctly stated, "'Faith' is not a general phenomenon in all religions; rather, *this central meaning was gained first in Christianity.*"[180]

180 Dieter Lührmann, "Faith," trans. Frank Witt Hughes, *Anchor Bible Dictionary*, eds. David Noel Freedman, Gary A. Herion, David F. Graf, John David Pleins (New York: Doubleday, 1992), 2:750, emphasis added.

DISCUSSION QUESTIONS

1. In what ancient city were the followers of Jesus Christ first called Christians?
2. Where in the New Testament is this information recorded?
3. What were some of the names Christ's followers were known by before they were referred to as Christians?
4. Although the name *Christian* appears in the New Testament, the appellation "the Christian faith" is not in the New Testament. Who apparently was the first Christian to use this appellation?
5. Who was the first Christian theologian to coin the name *Christianity*?
6. When in the Church's history did this theologian coin the name *Christianity*?
7. Although the appellation "the Christian faith" first appeared in the late fourth century, it became especially popular after the book *Der christliche Glaube* (The Christian Faith) appeared in the 1820s. What German theologian wrote that book?
8. Can you cite a post–New Testament document, widely used in churches, that refers to Christianity as the "symbol of the faith"?
9. When Christians say "the faith," what are they confessing or signifying by this appellation?

CHAPTER 7

EQUATING TODAY'S *BELIEF* WITH *FAITH*, ALSO A MISUSE OF FAITH

Dangers are no more light, if they once seem light; and more dangers have deceived men than forced them.

Francis Bacon, "Of Delays"

For quite some time, English-speaking Christians have used belief and faith as interchangeable, equivalent concepts; thus, both have been perceived and used as essentially conveying the same meaning. But is this still an accurate understanding? What do English speakers today understand or mean by *belief* and *faith*? This is an important question because the noun *belief* and its English verbal forms *believe*, *believed*, and *believing* no longer mean what they once meant in the distant past. This fact is not well-known, nor recognized today, in the English-speaking world, including among Christians.

Belief Gave Way to Faith

The second edition of the *Oxford English Dictionary* (*OED*) states,

> *Belief* was the earlier word for what is now commonly called *faith*. The latter originally meant in Eng. (as in OFrench) "loyalty to a person to whom one is bound by promise or duty, or to one's promise or duty itself," as in "to keep faith, to break faith," and the derivatives of *faithful, faithless*, in which there is no reference to "belief"; i.e. "faith" was = fidelity, fealty. But the word *faith* being through OF. *fei, feith*, the etymological representative of the L. *fides*, it began in the 14th c. to be used to translate the latter, and in the course of time, almost superseded "belief," esp. in theological language, leaving "belief" in great measure to the merely intellectual process or state. . . . Thus, "belief in God" no longer means as much as "faith in God."[181]

A few lines below this citation, the *OED* gives an example of the difference between *belief* and *faith* (noted in the final line of the above definition), using a line from William Wordsworth's 1814 poem *The Excursion*: "One in whom persuasion and belief Had ripened into faith."[182] This difference is also noted in Wilfred Cantwell Smith's book *Faith and Belief*.[183] According to Smith, when John Wycliffe first translated the Bible into Middle English from the Latin Vulgate in the fourteenth century, his earlier version used "*bilefe*, but in the later [version, 1382,] this is replaced at many

181 "belief, n.," *The Oxford English Dictionary*, second edition (Oxford: Clarendon Press, 1989), 782.

182 Ibid.

183 Wilfred Cantwell Smith, *Faith and Belief* (Princeton, NJ: Princeton University Press, 1979). I am indebted to Smith for having first made me aware of this important point.

points by the new word 'faith,' which was just beginning to come into use as the English form of the Latin *fides*."[184]

Given this background of how *faith* attained the former meaning of *belief*, which began in the fourteenth century, it is interesting that the third edition of the *OED* has since modified its earlier definition, removing the portion quoted above. Instead, the entry includes this etymology:

> The word [*belief*] shows considerable semantic overlap with the later French loan *faith* n. Especially in theological use, a distinction is frequently made between the two words, *belief* referring either to the intellectual assent to certain propositions or dogmas, or to the acceptance of the existence of God or another god, *faith* involving personal trust and commitment.[185]

Even though this modified entry notes there is "considerable . . . overlap" between *faith* and *belief*, it does still say a difference exists between the two words. However, the modified entry omits the concluding sentence that "'belief in God' no longer means as much as 'faith in God,'" even though it correctly conveyed the meaning of *pistis* (faith) in the New Testament.

The translators of the Authorized King James Version (AV) also recognized this shift, for in 1611 they adopted the change from "belief" to "faith" in all verses except one. The word *pistis* or its verbal forms appears 233 times in the Greek New Testament,

---

184 Ibid., 116.

185 "belief, n.," *OED Online* (Oxford University Press). The website notes that the entry for *belief* was fully revised in 2011 for the *OED* third edition.

and the AV correctly translates all of them except 2 Thessalonians 2:13. Here, the AV incorrectly translates *pistei aletheias* as "belief of the truth." But *pistei* (a verbal form of the noun *pistis*) in this passage does not mean "belief," as Wilfred Cantwell Smith has rightly noted. Yet, interestingly, most recent English Bibles, including the New King James Version and the English Standard Version, still translate *pistei aletheias* in this verse incorrectly as "belief in the truth" rather than "faith in the truth." The words "belief in the truth" in this passage indicate that English translators saw *faith* and *belief* as true synonyms, but in some instances, they are not, given that *belief* no longer has the meaning it had before *faith* assumed that meaning, as noted above.

The New American Standard Bible appears to be the only modern Bible that has broken away from the traditional, faulty translation of 2 Thessalonians 2:13. This version correctly translates *pistei aletheias* as "faith in the truth." Interestingly, Wycliffe's 1382 translation also has "in feith of treuthe," as does Luther's German New Testament translation of "*im Glauben der Wahrheit*" (faith in the truth).

Smith also contends that most Bible translations continue to use the noun *belief* and the verb *believe* as though these two words still mean what they meant before the fourteenth century. Then, they both meant, "to love, to hold dear, to cherish; conceptually, to recognize; actively, to entrust oneself to, to give one's heart, to make a commitment."[186] He argues that *belief* and *believe* in the English-speaking world have lost the former meaning in that both words now merely express a thought or a mere opinion, whether

186 Smith, *Faith and Belief*, 116–17.

right or wrong. Thus, when an individual, for example, says, "I *believe* we will have a cold winter this year," the person is expressing a mere thought or opinion. This statement is like saying, "I *think* we will have a cold winter this year." Saying "I believe" has now really replaced "I think," thus making "I think" synonymous with "I believe." Moreover, in addition to saying "I believe," which today commonly expresses a mere opinion, some analysts note that the word *believe* now tends to function as a word of noncommitment, for example, "I believe *that* there is a God," as opposed to "I believe *in* God." The latter statement indicates personal commitment; the former does not.[187]

Dropping *Belief* and *Believe*

As just indicated, today it is common to "believe" without having faith, for *believe* and *belief* are now essentially tantamount to holding certain ideas.[188] Thus, Smith has argued that *belief* and *believe* should be "dropped as religious concepts since they no longer refer directly to anything of human ultimacy."[189] He also contends that "belief, in the modern meaning of the word, has no place in the history of Christian thought. *The concept is not in the Bible.*"[190] Smith is correct to say *belief* is not in the Bible, for the only appearance of *belief* in most English Bibles is the result of incorrectly translating 2 Thessalonians 2:13 as "belief in the truth" instead of "faith in the truth." Smith also states, "The modern world has to

187 M. Colin Grant, "Faith and Belief," *The Iliff Review* (Winter, 1977), 22.

188 Smith, *Faith and Belief*, 12.

189 Ibid., 117.

190 Wilfred Cantwell Smith, *Belief and History* (Charlottesville: University Press of Virginia, 1977), 78.

rediscover what 'faith' means, and then to begin to talk about that; it must recover the verb to rediscover what it means to have faith, to be faithful, to care, to trust, to cherish, to be loyal, to commit oneself; to rediscover what 'believe' *used to mean*."[191]

Smith, however, does not indicate how the use of *faith*, which he says reflects personal faithfulness, caring, trusting, cherishing, loyalty, and commitment, can be rediscovered. He fails to note that the early Christians in the New Testament did have that kind of faith. That faith was the product of their having accepted the apostles' eyewitness accounts of the bodily resurrected Jesus Christ, who obtained for them life and salvation. To rediscover this faith, Christians today need to imitate the faith of the apostles and their followers, many of whom suffered and died for their faith during the first three centuries of the Roman persecutions. And as noted in chapter 1, here the words of William Henry Paine Hatch are relevant, for he has shown that faith (*pistis*) for the early Christians was "from the beginning much more than belief or conviction, for it involve[d] the feelings and the will as well as the intellect. Trust and loyalty [were] included in it."[192] This faith was "the basic principle of Christianity and the distinguishing characteristic of Christians."[193]

Believe In

It is important to underscore that "believing in" differs notably

---

191 Smith, *Faith and Belief*, 117.

192 William Henry Paine Hatch· *The Pauline Idea of Faith in Its Relation to Jewish and Hellenistic Religion* (Cambridge, MA: Harvard University Press, 1917), 35.

193 Ibid.

from "believing" without the preposition "in." For "believing in" (*pisteuo eis*), as found in the Greek of the New Testament, means putting one's faith *in* or *into* someone. Thus, in Acts 16:31, the apostle Paul and Silas told the fear-stricken jailer at Philippi, "*Believe in* the Lord Jesus, and you will be saved, you and your household" (emphasis added). To "believe in" someone reveals trust and commitment, which are two important aspects of a Christian's faith. Trust and commitment were what Jesus wanted His hearers to have when He told them, "Let not your hearts be troubled. *Believe in* God; believe also *in* Me" (John 14:1, emphases added). Jesus Christ is the object of His followers who "believed in" Him.

Thus, while "belief," "believe," "believed," and "believing" without the preposition "in" have lost much of their former theological significance, "believe in" does still retain its correct theological meaning of trust and commitment. When Christians today, for example, confess the Nicene Creed, they still rightly say, "I believe in one God, the Father the Almighty. . . . And in one Lord Jesus Christ. . . . And I believe in the Holy Spirit." The same is true when they confess the Apostles' Creed, whose three articles also begin with "I believe in." Hence, when Christians say, "I believe in" the Father, Son, and Holy Spirit, they are truly expressing their Christ-centered faith of trust and commitment in Him. To say "belief," "believe," and "believing" without the preposition "in" no longer conveys the same meaning. But it is not apparent that today's English-speaking Christians are consciously aware of this important reality.

The change in the meaning of "belief," "believe," and "believing" without the preposition "in," according to Smith, has been drifting away from the concept of "faith," and he faults the churches for having been unaware of this unfortunate reality. He even says a "modern heresy of the church is the heresy of believing. Not of believing this or that, but of believing as such. The view that to believe is of central significance—this is an aberration."[194] He contends it is the concept of "faith" that is biblically correct, not "belief," "believe," or "believing" without the preposition "in," as they are still commonly used and understood. He further states, "Faith is a radically divergent thing from belief. And it has become disastrous to confuse the two."[195]

Given that "belief," "believe," and "believing" no longer mean what they once meant, as shown above, how then can conscientious leaders of Christian churches today educate parishioners regarding this change in meaning so that their exclusive faith will be nurtured and enhanced? Thus, Christians should be taught to say "I believe in," rather than just saying "I believe" or "I believe that." Urging Christians to avoid merely saying "I believe," which is embedded in today's English-speaking culture, will facilitate this change. And whenever we Christians can use the word *faith* in place of the *belief*, we should strive to do so.

Mere Believing Can Obscure Knowing

Tim Keller, a Christian apologist of the Calvinist persuasion, mentions an interesting personal experience. As a Christian min-

194 Smith, *Belief and History*, v.

195 Ibid., 79.

ister, he said he believed that Jesus Christ rose bodily from the dead. And he added that he really did believe it, and it even gave him peace. Later, when diagnosed with thyroid cancer, he obtained N. T. Wright's book *The Resurrection of the Son of God* (2003). He soon began reading its eight hundred pages that scholarly and majestically defend Christ's bodily resurrection. "At the end of four weeks," Keller said, "I put it down . . . and I said, 'Oh my gosh, it really did happen.'"[196] Noteworthily, Keller had now moved from merely believing to authentically *knowing* that Christ had really risen bodily from the dead. Wright's book, interlaced with biblically irrefutable knowledge, convincingly underscored what Keller needed to *know*, which his "believing" previously did not accomplish. This interesting account further highlights the important role knowledge (*notitia* in Latin) has as a part of faith, discussed earlier in chapter 4.

An Additional Comment Concerning the English Word *Faith*

Given that the word *faith* now means what *belief* once meant, it is important to note the word *faith* in English has no verbal forms or cognates, unlike the Greek word *pistis*, which does have verbal forms. This requires English translators to use the word *belief* in place of *faith* and to use *believe*, *believing*, and *believed* as its verbal forms. It is the only way the verbal forms of *pistis* can be translated into English. Thus, English translators continue to use *belief*, even though *belief* no longer really imparts what *faith* now

196 Tim Keller's experience is partly abbreviated from his account, except his words that appear in quotation marks. Both are found in Justin W. Bass, *The Bedrock of Christianity* (Bellingham, WA: Lexham Press, 2020), 10.

conveys. Note the following familiar translation: "For we hold that one is *justified by faith* apart from works of the law" (Romans 3:28, emphasis added). But to translate this sentence as "For we hold one is *justified by belief* apart from the works of the law" does not impart the same theological meaning that the word *faith* conveys.

Conclusion

Given that the English word *faith* came to mean what *belief* once meant, we English-speaking Christians should use *faith* where we have in the past used the word *belief*. It is theologically more correct to say, "We have faith in God," than to say, "We believe in God." Similarly, we should strive to use the verb *believe* only with the preposition *in*. For we tend to say, "We Christians *believe* Christ, who said He will come to judge the living and the dead." But it would be more biblically correct to say, "We Christians *believe in* Christ, who said He will come to judge the living and the dead."

Thus, when a congregation in a formal church rite, for example, installs its officers, it is common for its pastor to ask them, "Do you believe the Apostles' Creed, the Nicene Creed, and the inspired Holy Scriptures?" To this question, the expected response is yes, and although this response sounds right, it is not quite correct, because the question was not correctly phrased. The pastor should have asked, "Do you *believe in* the Apostles' Creed, *in* the Nicene Creed, and *in* the inspired Holy Scriptures?" If the question had been asked in that manner, the answer of yes would have revealed commitment, whereas yes in response to the question of believing without the preposition *in* does not necessarily convey commitment. Hence, just as commitment was an important aspect of faith for the early Christians, Christians today need to indicate this same stalwart posture when making their confession of faith known to others where and whenever possible.

DISCUSSION QUESTIONS

1. Why do the concepts of belief and faith no longer convey the same meaning in English that they once had?
2. Why the difference in the meaning of *belief* and *faith* not well-known today?
3. Which fourteenth-century theologian translated the Bible into Middle English?
4. From what version or language did he translate the Bible?
5. In what year was the King James Version created?
6. What is another formal name for the King James Version?
7. Why do the words *belief* and *believe* no longer mean what they once meant theologically?
8. What is the difference between "believe" and "believe in"?
9. What is the difference between "believing" and "knowing"?

ACKNOWLEDGMENTS

This book would not have seen the light of day without the helpful support my loving wife, Carol, as she tolerated numerous hours spent in libraries and in my study at home, writing and rewriting, as well as read some of the book's early drafts.

Various aspects of this book were researched for about fifteen years in different libraries at educational institutions. I want to thank the library staff members at Concordia Seminary, St. Louis, particularly Lyle Buettner, Special Collections Librarian, and his present successor, Bruce Durazzi. Both provided some rare German and Latin volumes. My research efforts were also aided by the several library staff members at both Washington University, St. Louis, and St. Louis University, St. Louis.

Finally, I sincerely appreciate the time and devoted efforts of the staff at Concordia Publishing House, St. Louis, necessary to publish this book. I particularly have in mind the dedicated work of Jamie Moldenhauer, Laura Lane, Wayne Palmer, Tammy Bishop, Holli Rolfes, and Lindsey Scheetz.

INDEX

Faith community. Faith journey. People of faith. Faith leaders.

Have you ever heard or read these phrases? These and many other similar phrases are increasingly common, but what do they actually mean? In fact, what does *faith* mean?

While the word *faith* is often used today, rarely is it defined or even used correctly. *Faith Misused* goes back to the New Testament, examining the Greek word for *faith* and revealing how the Scriptures use the word in a radically different way than we do today. With that foundation in place, the rest of the book discusses how the Enlightenment affected modern usage of the word, explores how usage has changed since then, and gives examples of common misuses of the word *faith*.

Faith Misused will help Christians first to understand the true, biblical meaning of *faith* and then to use their words wisely to better portray that faith in a confused world.

Rev. Dr. Alvin J. Schmidt is professor of sociology emeritus at Illinois College in Jacksonville, Illinois, and a fellow of the Society for the Scientific Study of Religion. He is the author of numerous books, including the award-winning *Fraternal Organizations* (1980), *How Christianity Changed the World* (2004; now in eight different languages), and *Hallmarks of Lutheran Identity* (2017).

Concordia Publishing House
CPH.ORG

ISBN 978-0-7586-7111-0

9 780758 671110

RELIGION / Christian Life / Spiritual Growth
124637